WHAT OTHERS ARE SAYING AF

For everyone —whether you are in developing and developed countries—radical change and hypercompetition are accelerating, bringing greater stress into everyone's lives. People are burning out with exhaustion and future shock. Creative Living provides the only know antidote: the development of inner peace and a sense of self that keep people grounded as the world swirls around them. Read it and get centered so change and hypercompetition don't overwhelm you.

Richard d'Aveni, professor of Strategic Management at Dartmouth College and one of the world's top 50 business gurus. He is the author of *Hyper-competition ; Strategic Supremacy ; Beating the Commodity Trap: How Smart Companies Out-maneuver their Rivals to Win the Price War.*

* * * * *

In this clear and invigorating book, Dr. Arora calls for turning our lives to their source, our creativity, and offers ways to foster it and keep it alive.

Diana Balmori, award-winning urban and landscape designer, author, William Henry Bishop Visiting Professor of Architectural Design at Yale School of Architecture - Fall 2010, and Founder and Principal of Balmori Associates, New York.

* * * * *

For a long time I have known empirically that the best way to stimulate my scientific explorations was to explicitly carve out time for what are most often called creative activities—in my case it was building furniture. I will learn much from the author's precise and organized explanation of why I benefited so much.

Dr. David Pensak, scientific innovator, Creator of the first Internet firewall, global speaker, and who teaches at University of Princeton, University of Pennsylvania.

* * * * *

This self-help book that tells us not just 'what' to do, but rather how to do it. The author's approach to living using creative arts to improve the quality of our lives and our relations with others is unique. The style of the book blends practical insights with analytical tools. I have no doubt that readers will find the book to be highly instructive.

Anjini Kochar, Economist, who has taught at Stanford University and been a consultant to the World Bank. Currently India program director at Stanford.

* * * * *

Through her particular vantage point bridging the arts and the spirit, and the east and the west, Dr. Harbeen Arora provides an inspiring system to unlock the creative spirit in all of us. With warmth and wisdom, Dr. Arora leads the reader towards a transformative path of personal healing and growth. Through the ways of creative expression she clearly illustrates, you will not only gain insight and judgment, but an understanding of how to better orchestrate yourself to the universe around you. Dr. Arora shows us how the creative arts and the healing of mind, body, and spirit are as inextricably intertwined as our inseparableness from the world around us. A marvelous, truly global guide for people who want direct access to personal wellbeing and a more positive landscape of the people and community surrounding them. You will gain a deeper appreciation of the creative process, coupled with an understanding of how concrete steps can lead any individual to access personal expression, and how this new energy, in turn, will heal yourself, and the greater landscape of those around you.

Prof. Joshua Ronen teaches at the Stern School of Business, New York University. He is author of numerous books and articles in Accounting, Economics, Psychology and has published in the popular press (such as NYT)

CREATIVE LIVING

Discovering Your Beautiful Path and
Lifestyle toward Happiness and Well-being

HARBEEN ARORA, PhD

New York

Creative Living
Discovering Your Beautiful Path and Lifestyle Toward Happiness and Well-Being

ISBN 978-1-60037-736-5

Library of Congress Control Number: 2009941942

Morgan James Publishing
1225 Franklin Ave., STE 325
Garden City, NY 11530-1693
Toll Free 800-485-4943
www.MorganJamesPublishing.com

In an effort to support local communities, raise awareness and funds, Morgan James Publishing donates one percent of all book sales for the life of each book to Habitat for Humanity. Get involved today, visit **www.HelpHabitatForHumanity.org**.

Contents

Part I: SEEING
Sorting Your Mind:
Interacting With Your Visual Space

Part II: BEING
Strengthening Your Relationships:
Playing And Progressing In The Theater Of Life

Part III: CREATING
Engaging Your Soul:
Harnessing The Power Of Sound And Music

DEDICATION

I dedicate this book to that caring and guiding hand of the universe whose presence I felt throughout writing it. In choosing me as the medium of this work, it helped me to become one with its message.

I also dedicate this work to my guide and mentor, Vinay Rai. His faith in me was much more than my faith in myself. Each time I floundered in courage or had doubts about my own abilities, he was there for me with his reassuring words and deep wisdom. I have learned my first lessons in creative living from him. His caring heart, undying courage and sincere friendship have guided me and my search for myself.

Vinay is an inspiration for many young people I know. We all see in him a valiant crusader who stands up for causes and people he believes in. We seek his solid advice to sort ourselves in moments of confusion and crisis. We admire his great capacity for meeting all sorts of challenges, without losing his calm. As he says, "Life was not meant to be easy, because we weren't meant to be lazy!"

What I find truly remarkable is his guileless and genuine way of relating to everyone—be that a man on the street, a high office bearer, or a business rival. Looking at his example, I realized that our learning and wisdom are meant to come alive in our day to day thinking and conduct.

Finally, I dedicate this book to all of you. May you find your harmonious path toward peace and progress as surely as I have found mine.

FOREWORD

—By Vinay Rai

I am absolutely sure you will enjoy reading this book. This is because the book has emerged from the true story of Harbeen herself—her path of seeking her happiness and her discovery of her own self with all the beauty and love her spirit is capable of. You will relate to her journey all the more since Harbeen is like anyone of you out there—similar issues, problems, fears, stresses, challenges, and difficulties.

All that you need to start with, like Harbeen, is a genuine wish to live life to its fullest and respond positively to challenges. And believe me, Harbeen has had a mouthful of them (including her stint at the University of Paris, where she literally lived on ten dollars a month and had to do her thesis in French, without knowing earlier even a word of that language!). Throughout, she kept her faith in a higher power, never for a moment doubting that positive openings were hidden in its unfathomable ways.

And then in her journey of this book, she rediscovered what she unconsciously knew. That you cannot change the environment or the people around you, but you can change your own outlook. This way you will find your happiness and thus positively influence your environment.

My own life's journey has in many ways been quite a roller coaster with its fair, perhaps too much, share of ups and downs. I too, like many of you out there, had risen to dizzy heights in business and fame and then fallen. Yet at no point did I give up on my faith, resilience, courage and positive vision. As a result, I moved ahead and rose again. I can thus say with authority that you can remain completely happy, content and at peace with yourself, by not letting the many trials of life touch you negatively.

In any case, your highs and lows are an integral part of your learning process. So never for a moment blame anyone or feel disgusted. In my sixty years of life, I have lived and learned that you can transform a moment of suffering into one of strength by your own inspired thinking. This book incorporates many of my own approaches that I have tried and tested.

Harbeen's sensitive awareness, her affectionate nature, her desire to meet challenges to the best of her ability, her habit of questioning herself, and her genuine interest in solving problems for herself and others have all contributed significantly to this inspiring yet practical approach of creative living. Importantly, her own personal learning curve during the writing this book—her ups and downs, highs and lows, but essentially, her "discovery of her own self"—makes this work an almost autobiographical one. At the close of her adventure with this book, rather her sacred pilgrimage, her transformation was evident.

This book will help you likewise to rediscover and reinvent yourself. It's a beautiful self-satisfying journey, irrespective of where you reach. Read through this book with an open mind. Assimilate the warmth and energy that Harbeen radiates. Try out her suggestions with trust in her vision and faith in yourself.

Happy reading, and more importantly, happy imbibing!

Vinay Rai is the president of the Rai Foundation, a philanthropist, and author of *Think India: The Rise of the World's Next Superpower and What It Means for Every American* (published by Dutton, Penguin Group, U.S.A, 2007).

The greatest part of our happiness depends on our dispositions, not our circumstances.
—Martha Washington

INTRODUCTION

CREATIVE LIVING: ENCHANTING YOURSELF INTO HAPPINESS AND WELL-BEING

The way of creative living will restore to your life its birthright—its fullness and enduring happiness, something most of us are falling short of, even when we are inherently capable of attaining it.

Creative living is about having creative attitudes. Equipped with them, you can turn your bad moods into good ones, feel stronger within, and respond positively to all kinds of situations. Creative living is then about assuming leadership of your life and leading it to happiness.

This book is not just for those who are 'depressed.' All of us are depressed in some ways! As Buddhist scholar Allan Wallace says, even a normal person is "subject to many types of mental distress, including anxiety, frustration, restlessness, boredom, and resentment."[1] Such ways of being and behaving sap your vitality and deplete your creativity. You need to rise above them, or simply have the willingness to do so. This book will be your friend and guide in this endeavor. Creative living will help you to clarify your mind and simplify your life. It will stimulate you to think and act with your better nature. It will help you to will your happiness and warrant it as well.

A THREE-FOLD PATH AND LIFESTYLE
TO COACH YOUR CREATIVITY

In her book, *The Creative Brain,* Nancy C. Andreasen informs us of creative attitudes that are common to creative people in a variety of spheres from literature to leadership. These are: openness to experience, adventuresomeness, rebelliousness (as in rejection of dogmatic thinking and zeal to do things differently), individualism, sensitivity, playfulness, persistence, curiosity, and simplicity.[2] Such attributes are innate in all of you. You just need to spur them through suitable design. The three-fold path of creative living is one such framework.

As I see it, your well-being is uplifted by three factors: your personal positive thoughts and feelings, your strong and supportive interpersonal relationships, and your ability to be in tune with your larger environment. My modus is to energize all these three levels of your being and well-being.

Interestingly, in the simple mantra *"Aum Shanti Shanti Shanti"* (that some of you may be familiar with), the word *Shanti,* meaning peace, is recited thrice over. It is for a reason. This mantra is a prayer asking for peace in three different realms of your living: individual, interpersonal, and universal. I seek to connect you positively and plentifully to all three levels. Synergy in this triad will sustain your creative force.

For this purpose, I employ the creative opportunities innate in the three ordinary realms that surround you—the visual-material space, the theater of relationships and the vibrational environment. Now you are part of all of them at all moments. But do you relate to them with awareness? When you look at any place or thing, do you look deep enough, close enough and care enough to wonder and ask questions? *Do you energize your imagination thus?* Or when you are in a group of people, are you sensitive to the prejudices, biases, and ego games in the air? *Do you energize your role and play thus?* Or when you are in any situation, can you sense the delicate and ever-shifting vibrational state of your inner and outer worlds? *Do you energize your influence thus?*

With your greater awareness and intimate rapport with these three realms, you will in effect exercise your thoughts, behavior and actions. You will then see, feel, hear, conduct and create in more positive and creative ways. Basically, as your inner world starts looking up, your rapport with your outer world will be transformed. You will relate to your life with much more light in your head and love in your heart.

Creative living will take you on a journey of self-discovery. It will make you rethink who you are and help you to redo your habits. Now just being born human does not make one humane; no more than possessing a car makes one a good driver. Therefore, we all need guidance and pointers to learn how to navigate the complex field of life. And then it will look quite simple!

EXPANSIVE ATTITUDES FOR CREATIVE VITALITY

In apparent contradiction to my premise of creative thinking being an energizing force, a study indicates that people in creative arts have a high degree of depression! A study done in 1995 "found a lifetime prevalence of depression of 50% for people working in the creative arts… Particularly vulnerable to depression were writers of poetry (77%) and fiction (59%) and visual artists (50%)".[3] Then, what makes me propose that a creative lifestyle will help you not just beat the blues, but also energize yourself? Are we missing out on something?

Yes—the way in which we understand 'creativity'. Currently in the west, we think of creativity as emerging from the individual. When we think of creativity as something coming from us or that we can control, we risk becoming self-conscious, as we want to be admired and respected for what we say or do. Or we become fearful or 'go crazy' as we are unable to fathom all that we generate on the path of creative exploration. Or we become arrogant and closed to new influences upon tasting the slightest success. Ergo, when we see ourselves as creative agents, the many facets of our ego come into play and stand in the way of our expansion.

In the east however, creativity is seen as an inspired consciousness that you access when you are relaxed and at peace with yourself. But to be restful likewise and thus express with true freedom, you are required to take yourself a little less seriously! You need to see yourself as a creative medium and not as the creator. Only then will you open yourself to your own depths and tap into the creative forces all around.

To take my personal instance, from the day I began writing this book—my first one—I prayed to the universe to guide my path. To release myself of my own expectations, I admitted that I needed help and I accepted that my intelligence wasn't enough. Every morning, with folded hands and a humble heart, I would ask the universe's music to flow through me, using me as its medium. This stance also led me to feel that my responsibility was shared (by the universe) and that I could just propose whatever I wanted and it would be checked and balanced by its larger intelligence. Released thus from my self-consciousness, I allowed my sincere feelings to flow into my writing. At the end of the day, I felt satisfied, not because I'd written a good piece, but simply because I'd worked to the best of my ability. If my work seemed good, I would thank the universe. If it didn't, I'd pass of the buck to it!

I speak about many such ennobling stances that are enabling as well. I find my inspiration from proverbial wisdom and delightful fables from all over the world, and especially Indian philosophy as espoused in the Vedanta. The latter, in a nutshell, is about taking responsibility for your happiness and expanding yourself steadily from a unitary being to a unified one. It's a journey from 'I-to-You-to-Us'. And you accomplish it through a steady and conscious process of harmonizing and integrating. That is what this book is all about.

WHAT THE CHAPTERS CONTAIN AND
WHAT YOU WILL TAKE AWAY

Briefly, the first part of the book aims to help you see better. You will develop here a more sensitive awareness of your visual and tactile realm. The visual realm is used to heighten your awareness and foster your initiative. It's a site of stress busting, healing and reorganizing the furniture in your mind. It will also keep your hands active and engaged. And when you're busy, you can't be bothered!

Yet indifference doesn't drive creativity. Contact and care do. So the second part of my book is about ways to engage in a positive ways with the perplexing theater of interpersonal relationships, which are replete with different characters and challenging situations. I offer ways to witness such daily interactions, and use their myriad mirrors to reflect upon ourselves. You will soon come to realize, as I have, that this world and its daily struggles are in fact testing grounds for strengthening our own balance and chiseling our own creative self. So just like the proverbial lotus thrives in muddy waters, you too will awaken and unfold because of your difficult relationships and situations—and your positive handling of them. This section will help you to behave and relate better.

The final section is about engaging the power of sound and silence to awaken your innate musical sensibility. You will thus have a greater sense of harmony and symphony in different spheres of your life. It will help you to respond and create better.

All sections stimulate you similarly, using different means. They all help you channel your negative energies, lift your mood, clear your mind, warm your heart, cool your head, curtail your ego, improve your behavior and inspire your actions.

But for creative living to become your second nature, you need to make a lifestyle out of it, just like to maintain your health, you need to make good eating and exercise a way of life.

HEAL YOURSELF TO HEAL THE WORLD

Perhaps you are still wondering at the "impracticality" of my premise for various reasons. A physician listening to my premise of healing through creativity observed wryly, "The answer to pain is in a pill, not in a painting." Indeed! Creative living simply aims to pre-empt the daily hurts, headaches and heartbreaks that give rise to all kinds of health travails in the long run. Doctors are increasingly emphasizing the energizing role of positive thinking, will power, laughter, light-heartedness, and forgiveness in order to reduce the cumulative negative effects of day-to-day feelings of bitterness, annoyance, impatience and anger.

Now upon this path, it is not as if you won't have your highs and lows. It is just that now you will know what to do with them! In fact, with positive habits of handling problems, your highs and lows will become stepping stones to your creativity: every negative emotion can help you to become all the more positive.

You may still doubt my optimism for yet another reason. The increasing aggression in society, negative behavior among colleagues and even friends, lack of values, loss of integrity, artificiality in social exchanges et al are fostering mistrust and misdemeanor all around us. Indeed, good standards of conduct are less visible in our times. Or are they?

Don't we see the negative more because we magnify it in our mind? Yes, indeed. We pay more attention to negative behavior and ignore positive stories and examples. So what we are actually doing is akin to this: we are always looking at those who score low on tests of humanity instead of drawing inspiration from those who score higher. Behold the blunder!

The real problem in our lives is not so much of increasing negativity, but of weakened creativity. Most of us law-abiding and peace-loving people aren't working consciously and concertedly enough to bring good things to life and into our life. This book will show you how to help yourself and your world, by just uplifting the way you see, behave and relate.

Finally, this book is just another milestone in our shared and eternal quest of how to be and what to do. Take and test what speaks to you. Arrive at your own insights. Creative living by definition is a work in eternal progress. Keep adding new layers to it. To start, accept my sincere and sacred offering to your journey of awakening. It has changed my life. It will transform yours.

PART I: SEEING

Sorting Your Mind:
Interacting with Your Visual Space

Vision is the primary medium of thought.
—Rudolf Arnheim[1]

CHAPTER 1
SUMMONING YOUR VISUAL WORLD

Today, as in yesteryears, humans express themselves through color, form and design. With their aid, our inner jumble of energies becomes clear and visible to us. In India, we are famous for visualization of millions of gods even though we consider god to be a single and unified energy. The diverse forms are simply ways to help us fathom our vast reality in visible ways. So when you create an image embodying some aspects of your greater reality, you make it easy for yourself to grasp it. To take from what Swami Vivekananda says, just like you need "cups" to hold water and drink it in an easier way,[2] so do you need images to hold your many ideas and understand them in holistic ways.

Your greater visual awareness and engagement will stimulate your thinking to become more compact and concrete. It will further sharpen your powers of observation, trigger your initiative and inventiveness, make you open to change, enhance your communication, and tap into your ability to visualize positive realities and create them too. It will eventually help you to see possibilities in the midst of trouble and find solutions where none seem apparent. You will see from the right side of life.

IMAGES: INSIDE, OUTSIDE

Your world is visual. So are your thoughts. Rudolf Arnheim in his seminal book *Visual Thinking* says: "Thinking calls for images and images contain thought."[3] Your feelings are colorful too. You could be feeling the blues on Monday morning or going green at the news of your colleague's promotion. You also understand a concept better when someone puts it visually for you, using a map or metaphor. Your memory too is based on graphic structures of association. Some people in India can repeat the 1,008 different names of a deity just from their memory. I would often wonder how they could memorize it all! A closer look revealed that these multiple names were a bit like acronyms: they looked small but contained a list of associations. Let's say one name could mean "daughter of so and so" or another could suggest "white and radiant like the moon" or "one who rides a tiger." As you can see, each name paints a picture. And your brain needs just that for better recall and memory.

In an experiment, psychologists showed subjects one thousand photographs in succession. Thereafter, they mixed one hundred new photos with the older ones, asking subjects to point out those they had not seen earlier. It is amazing that everyone remembered exactly which photo had been seen earlier and which ones had been inserted later.[4] So you can forget a name but not a face!

Your eyes are equipped for graphic observation. They can take amounts of light that would make deep-sea fish go blind.[5] Your day vision is sharper than that of a cat or dog. You have a superior eye for detail, pattern, and color. Unlike giant anteaters, for which smell points the way, or for bats, for which sound is a greater guide, for you seeing is indeed believing.

Businesses know that! In a market study of what consumers respond most to while making purchases, a whopping 92.6 percent placed primacy on visual parameters.[6] Actually, you do the same! When making choices about whom to trust or where to put your money, you go by the looks. In employee interviews, observations mostly occur in visual terms (e.g., "he looks sincere," "doesn't look reliable," "let me give his CV a good look"). Even in interpersonal interactions, what you see in people or about them forms your lasting opinion.

In fact, you ascribe great value to what you see with your own eyes and also to what you see in another's eyes. Body-language experts suggest that non-verbal signals emanating from the eyes are "the most revealing and accurate of all" communication signals. First, because "they are a focal point on the body" and second, your "pupils work independently of conscious control."[7] Which means your eyes will include information that your words might omit. Also, steady eye contact and smiling eyes—when your smile reaches the eyes—signal genuine behavior.[8] Trust, therefore, is deeply connected to satisfying visual interactions. But don't jump to conclusions if someone looks away while talking. It could be because your good looks are distracting him or her![9]

Even your overall body language and behavior are visible markers of your psyche and intentions. The famous Mehrabian's rule states that only 7 percent of communication is verbal, while 93 percent is non verbal, comprising 38 percent of vocal cues, like tone and inflection, and 55 percent of visual signals, like facial expressions, posture, and demeanor. Your graphic gestures—moves, facial expressions, overall behavior and actions—communicate at a vital and visceral level.

More cognition comes from visual inputs. What you see informs your brain the most; a tier of the brain's volume (over 35 percent) is taken up by visual regions.[10] The vision has more neurons working for it.[11]

However, visual experience is intensified and enhanced through the integrated action of all your senses. Try watching a film with the sound muted and buttered popcorn out of reach! Without the background music guiding your attention, you won't understand how you're supposed to look at a certain character and feel about their actions.

Sounds speak to your heart, visuals speak to your head, and butter speaks to your tongue. You then need to look after the health of all!

It is just that in case of conflict among sensory inputs, the visual ones reign. So if the vocal tone of your colleague tells you that she is nice and sweet but if upon meeting her you find her eyes and expressions as unreliable, you'll believe what you see.

That is why visuals make good warnings. They give you the bigger picture in lesser time and are quickly picked up by your brain. In the book *Visual Selling,* the authors suggest that visual warnings provide a compelling picture of context and consequences. They give a vision of things to come and thus beget greater attention and adherence.[12] Taking cue, most countries now mandate that cigarette packs should carry visual warnings in addition to the verbal.

Moreover, when you see a negative consequence of a product or action, you become much more wary of it. That is why many schools now mandate that young students visit de-addiction and trauma centers as part of their curriculum in order to see and understand the far-reaching consequences of alcohol abuse or drunken driving. When you see someone who suffered brain injuries in an accident resulting from drunken driving, or hear stories of lives lost, you are dissuaded from repeating those mistakes. Instead, you learn positive lessons from them.

For similar reasons, analogies make good examples. Metaphors and stories help you see the essence of a situation. You have more empathy when can actually see someone's predicament through a telling narration or an actual visual. A girl once told me how her boyfriend could not understand her fears when a man was repeatedly stalking her. Only when he saw the video footage caught on the TV camera did he fully visualize and realize the emotional impact of that event.

So when others can't see it the way you do, you just need to make them see it more graphically. Consciously choreographed communication will help you engage another's imagination more effectively. This is not to say that you shouldn't speak from your heart or discourage spontaneity. But painting a fuller picture around the theme will make your ideas more visible and graspable. To make your communication visually stimulating, give your brain more visual stationary to play with. Employ ample analogies and metaphors to get your point across. Paint pictures. Create scenarios. Tell stories.

"The brain absorbs a lot more information when it's presented in pictures rather than in stacks of data from a computer,"[13] says a scientist at Tufts University. Research shows that extensive use of visual aids and mnemonic (memory-enhancing) techniques, for example using symbols, colors, pictures, metaphors, acronyms, comparisons, cross-referencing, and rhyming, helps strengthen connections between the brain's neurons, creating memory, triggering recall and enhancing communication.

Finally, an image creates emphasis. And your attention flows easily toward where there is emphasis. So empower your pursuit of your goals by visualizing them as concrete images. What you behold is what you uphold! Likewise, visualize your role models. Studies tell us that when we look up to someone, we easily imbibe their characteristics.[14] Stir your imagination by imitating them. Behave as if they would have. Enter this larger role. You'll exit your limited one.

Of course, your choice of a particular role model will also reveal to you the values that you sub-consciously espouse. This self-awareness is crucial.

EXPLORING YOUR SUBCONSCIOUS

Just like the food you eat gives your body certain properties, likewise the images circulating in your sub-conscious mind give it a peculiar chemistry. But this chemistry is ever changing and can be reset, as it is responsive to how you imagine, depending on your thoughts and exposure. Expose yourself to a couple of evenings of mindless television programming or allow yourself to think negatively and you'll find a lot of inertia building in your imagination. On the other hand, immerse yourself in the wild over a weekend or spend time in enlightened company and your senses will be uplifted by a much more positive subconscious orientation.

Of course, apart from day to day changes in your mood or environment, your subconscious is also deeply marked by your individual experiences, habits, upbringing, education, culture and values. If you've been brought up in a secure and stable house, the word 'parents' will conjure a very different image for you than it would for an orphan.[15] Likewise, if you are from the East, you will hear the phrase 'a silent day' with positive associations, even with spiritual overtones, while a Westerner may equate it with loneliness. [16]

Your negative mental associations can be reset in positive ways, provided you can see them clearly. There are exciting exercises in art therapy to confront your inner images. Art therapist Ikuko Acosta at NYU shared with me some exercises. For instance, how you draw a door can reveal how you relate to the outside world. Door ajar signals openness while a locked one tells of a more guarded stance. What's further interesting is that Indian students, she found, would draw embellished and ornate doors, in tune with their cultural upbringing of hospitality, whilst American students would draw them with locks, in accord with the heightened sense of privacy in their part of the world.[17] You can also discover your inner world by watching yourself play with objects around you. How do you place the flowerpots in your garden? Do you prefer to place them in orderly lines or random curves? How do you like to place cutlery on the dinner table? Do you make interesting arrangements with spoons and forks or do you simple pile them up?

In fact, even in art therapy, the process of exploration is seen to be as important, perhaps more, than what the final picture says. As art therapist Ruth Abraham says, "Preferences in composition, choice of color, attraction to specific materials, and rhythm of lines are all ways of sharing perceptions and inner life."[18] For instance, I usually choose crayons or poster colors when painting because they dry faster!

Analysis, however, should be the last thing on your mind when you sketch on a paper, lay the table, or give your garden a new look. Don't be in a hurry to find meaning in every mood! Let some moods be! It's more important to absorb yourself in visually engaging activities for enabling inner reorganization. You can observe your patterns as well, but do so over a period of time rather than look for quick-fix judgments. Sorting your inner space should not make you rigid. It should help you lead yourself toward more vitality and variety in your inner space. For that, you need time to express yourself in exploratory ways. So the more important thing, as author and art therapist Shaun McNiff says, is "to trust the process," of creating anything in your visual realm, with the belief "that something valuable will emerge when we step into the unknown."[19]

By exploring your inner energies through the visual medium, you will enhance your self-awareness. You can then use this precious information to remodel your energies in the direction of your dreams. However, realization of your dreams depends on your ability to discipline your energies. Because your mind influences how your material shapes up!

So use the visual space to inspire your thoughts and actions, especially in areas where you find yourself challenged.

RESOLVE, REMIND—PAVING THE WAY FOR POSITIVE HABITS

Visual reminders do a great job of shifting you to new habits, helping you imbibe them fully, not wishfully. If you have a problem containing your anger, make a picture of the consequences of anger, like your spouse walking out on you or wrinkles being added to your face every time you frown (whatever scares you more!). However, in crafting reminders to yourself or instructions to others, affirm your thoughts in positive ways. The brain responds much more when told, and shown, "what to do."[20] So instead of telling yourself/others "not to get angry," urge yourself or others to smile more. Back it with a good reason to create an image of your instruction for better recall and motivation. Tell yourself or others that smiling gives a glow to the face or that it attracts the goddess of wealth!

Also, when you tell your mind what to, you give it a positive goal to pursue. It knows what to do next. Your brain works best in action. Analysis is best left to your conscience. (We'll come that later.) So instead of telling yourself to avoid junk food, tell yourself to eat more of fruits and cereal. Your brain will start chasing the new positive goal and forget all else. In a similar vein, a friend of mine once told me that when she goes on a fast from speech, she directs her brain 'to sing' instead of asking it 'not to speak.' If she does the latter, her brain speaks all the more!

In sports psychology, it is observed that racing drivers who tend to look for negative possibilities in effect end up finding them, either falling or going off-track all that much more.[21] So if you think something will go wrong, it probably will. So even as your recognize your limitations, remain focused on your possibilities. That is the only way to empower your individual agency—strengthen your ability to create something out of nothing.

Indeed, the more you think negative, the more you imagine negatively. Although exaggerating one's fears is a Zen technique to see them as ridiculous and thus release them, for some people such amplification magnifies their fears. For this reason, art therapist Frances F. Kaplan warns that excessive exposure to or unchecked creation of "emotion-laden images" can in fact "intensify unpleasant feelings."[22] Little wonder that most people prefer to buy art that spurs positive feelings or helps them relax.[23] We all want to feel good at the end of the day.

However, you needn't run away from negative images. Life is a mixed bag. The feel-good comes together with the disconcerting. But even negative pictures can stimulate you in positive ways. It's how you process them. I know someone who keeps a wartime picture of a small dead child in the rubble with open, piercing eyes. He entitles it as: "Care for life. It's easily lost." He says that while driving or at work, if he feels like retorting impatiently to angrily, he takes a good look at this picture. Greater acts of violence come from smaller acts of violence in our daily loves. Images that remind us of our follies and correct us in good time, or even a little later, can prevent us from repeating them. Mindfulness of what can go wrong can in fact help us make the right choices.

So while the feel-good is comforting, the feel-bad can be a crucial trigger for positive thinking and action. So displace and disorient yourself consciously. Venture out to see how the homeless live. Visit a hospital to behold the sight of the sick: you will return home with deeper reflections on life and mortality. To make sense of your own life's journey, see some other journeys.

You just need to be aware that negative images, if stuck in your head, can foster undue fears. I remember that as kids we were very scared to venture out of our rooms if we had just seen ghost story. Your personal fears make you hallucinate all the more! So you too might see a bleeding person when you visit the hospital and that image may create anxiety. An instant remedy is to have a change of scene. Go out in the sun. Look at some family pictures. Play soothing music. See some friends. Distraction is therapeutic as well.

To counter negative feelings at all times, develop some perennial positive practices. Use spaces within your reach, like cupboards, walls, or gadgets, the way a marketer would use them—as advertising opportunities to sell dreams of happiness. In such a climate of feel-goodness, you will certainly find the motivation to process negative feelings in positive ways. Post a peppy message on your fridge door and pause to reflect at it every time you open it. Or place a map of your blessings on your kitchen wall so that you can see it while you cook. You will cook with a lot more inspiration!

At another level, energize yourself through ordinary objects. One way is to mint value from the symbolic associations of some objects you possess. Maybe you have a ring that belongs to your great grandmother and wearing it makes you feel connected to your roots. Or you may have a college-time souvenir that brings back memories of fun times or reminds you of your achievements. Bring these powerful pieces out of the closet! A friend of mine, rather mild and mellow otherwise, keeps in her purse this embroidered handkerchief that was gifted to her by her best friend many years ago. She says that just having that handkerchief, reminder of a powerful bond with her friend, helps her find her courage in moments when she needs it. Objects with symbolic meaning can exert a powerful force on our psyche. They help allay our anxieties, collect our scattered thinking, and help us feel secure and confident. Fill up your house or work-cabin or vehicle or with them. Look at them. Talk to them. Turn them into your daily deities.

Invest your ordinary possessions with extraordinary associations through your active imagination. For instance, pick up that book you really like. Think of who gave it to you. Thank this person for his or her good gesture. Look at this book as a precious guide. Strangely, it will start playing that role. Likewise, when making a cup of tea for your spouse, dedicate the act of stirring in the sugar to his well-being. Your spouse will feel the intensity of your feelings too.

Basically, when you invest ordinary spaces and occasions with more feeling, you become more dedicated to the task at hand and in turn it begins to energize you.

SPACES, SENSATIONS AND SMART MOVES

Your behavior responds to space. A well-lit room with windows and a good of view will comfort you more than the one that looks damp and dark. Likewise, a clean space will stimulate thoughtful action while a cluttered space will increase your confusion. A frequent visitor to India observed that people traveling in the New Delhi Metro were more courteous as compared to those who traveled in crowded buses. In effect, the travelers are the same in both cases. Only their sensibilities are different in response to the different spaces.

Organizations have already begun to use design to foster positive interactions. Indeed, more communication can be encouraged or discouraged through space settings, or power equations can be emphasized or underplayed through strategic design. One company removed departmental partitions and introduced mobile furniture that staff could roll across. This minor innovation ended up bringing major changes in the way departments communicated. The mobile furniture gave them the impulse of contact and experimentation, and the disparate departments began to engage a lot more from then on. Architect Jeff Scherer considers that the design of a space can help "unlock the spiritual side of the individual," increasing the person's performance and productivity.[24]

Studies show us how seating arrangements determine who you end up addressing. In a meeting, you will tend to address the person seated across you more, as compared to the one sitting right next to you. (No wonder the frontbenchers are asked more questions!) But if it were a huge table, you would prefer to address the one sitting next to you.[25] In conversations, the more you like someone, the more you will turn your chair or stance toward them. It also means that when the going is not so gung-ho between two people, just turning toward one another can help foster trust and warmth. Interestingly, spatial preferences are gender-sensitive. In general, men seem to be are attracted by solidity and cavities while women are attracted by curves, protrusions and embellishments.[26] Men like it simple, women like it special. Don't we know!

But some colors and spatial settings work positively for all. In the United States, jails are being suffused with pastel pinks to help inmates relax, resulting in less violent behavior.[27] In shelter homes too, the walls tend to have colors to relax or energize (pink/blue or lime/orange respectively). In terms of spatial dynamics, circular arrangements usually encourage more receptive and respectful exchange.

Become alert to how your space is structuring power relations and affecting exchange. Use your awareness to make smart moves. For instance, in India, you choose to sit at the feet of elders, even though this gives the high pedestal to the other. But you deliberately choose this unequal setting to show your respect toward your elders and invoke their blessings. At a subliminal level, this strategic subservience helps you to accept the superiority of your elders and helps them to keep their competitive urges at bay. Of course, at times, for the one who is looking down at you, the illusion of being superior might get to his or her head! But never mind. At least, in looking up, you get to keep your chin up!

In fact, adopt the subservient position by choice in cases where you already are in a position of power. The lower level will check your exploitative use of power and the higher level will help your subordinate to be more expressive.

On a similar note, a senior citizen once observed that living in small and shared spaces increased one's inclination to resolve interpersonal conflicts. The fact that all had to return to the same room at the end of the day ensured that the members made up quickly and resolved playfully. He lamented that with modern insular living, where young people having no compulsion to share with others, our attitudes risk becoming rigid and inflexible. See if you can make use of this in your home!

Use the many enabling spaces in nature to heal yourself. Take energy from the elements to get back into your element! In fact, not just the scenic aspect but also the sheer scale of natural spaces can uplift your vision. For instance, experiencing the immensity of an ocean or the majesty of mountains can make you feel differently and thus see differently. "Perhaps it was the size and height of the mountains that made me feel that there were deeper and more powerful forces at work in organizations,"[28] observes Larry E. Greiner, a professor of business, while reflecting over his subject.

In the presence of over-awing spaces—so many in nature—it becomes easier for you to have a shift of awareness, to get the larger picture, to break through old patterns of thinking and behavior. So take frequent vacations! Such places are in fact freely available to us. Just look up to the vast expanse of the sky, the moving clouds during day and the beautiful star-studded universe at night. Behold the miracle of nature. Become wide-eyed once again. See with wonder to counter your weariness and wariness.

As you move out to energizing spaces, come home to one too. Have more thoughtful and artful arrangements in your home and purview. Importantly, fashion your home in the image of what you would want to be. As author of *Creativity*, Mihaly Cziksentmihaly aptly observes that "having a home (or a space) that reinforces one's individuality cannot but help increase the chances that one will act out of one's uniqueness."[29] Rhonda Byrne in *The Secret* suggests making a "Vision Board" wherein you "place pictures of all the things you want, and pictures of how you want your life to be."[30] Create, as writer Juhani

Pallasma says, a "caring environment," to offer yourself and others one "a safe place" that engenders "experiences of life and hope."[31]

The visual language of colors and coordination heightens our awareness and energizes our feelings. This hospital in Sweden renovated its facilities for patients with senile dementia to create an environment that was beautiful, elegant, with a design replete of the era when they lived young and healthy lives. They would now get their meals served in coordinated cutlery in porcelain and not plastic. The hospital felt like a fine-dining restaurant! These changes injected more warmth and hope in the lives of the patients as well as improved their relationship with other patients, and also staff. They all would even eat together. Results showed that these cosmetic changes were rather curative as "patients became happier and more susceptible to social contacts and their dietary intake increased considerably."[32]

Use visual means to make your feelings more evident and recallable. So the next time you say sorry to someone, offer along with a humble flower. Gestures linger longer than words. Or when you serve your grandparents dinner, use that china that you reserve for special occasions. They will receive your love. And in caring for others, you will feel cured as well.

Now when it comes to caring, the drama is in the details. The small gestures can fetch you disproportionate respect and love from the other. So when you drop off your male colleague today after work, make the gesture of dropping him at his doorstep, instead of leaving him on the street. Of course, he'll offer. But don't take the offer! He is doing what he thinks will give you least trouble, but you must also think about what will make him happier. In his place, what would make you happy? Yes, the drop at the doorstep! And frankly, if you've come all this way, you might as well go a little further. Believe me that an inch of care will make a mile of a difference to your relationship. In this case, you will now say bye-bye like brothers.

Finally, you will notice that your hands play a central role in making meaningful use of your material realm. After all, you need to hold objects and handle spaces. Let's see what all happens inside you when you use your hands in external spheres.

ENGAGE YOUR HANDS: FOR COOLER HEADS, WARMER HEARTS, AND INVENTIVE THINKING

"When the hand ceases to scatter, the heart ceases to pray," as says an Irish proverb. There is an intimate connection between your hands and your heart. The more you use your hands to help yourself and others, the more you allow your heart to come into play and thus mellow your thinking and behavior.

To stimulate your heart, give whatever you can, whenever you can. A gesture of care and concern in any given moment—a smile, a helping hand, a concerned query, patient listening, sincere understanding, bringing cheer and laughter, giving hope—all create tremendous energy in you and others. Through conscious gestures of giving (anything positive) you expand your spirit, connect to another and uplift your playing field. Moreover, as you energize others, you heal yourself as well. Giving is thus gratifying even in the absence of any return or reward.

The visual space engages your hands heartily. So keep your hands busy with even seemingly routine tasks, like arranging books on the shelf, sorting cutlery on your food tray in a flight, ironing your dress, polishing your car, picking up pieces of paper lying on your office floor, giving a reassuring touch to your friend, making coffee for your colleague, or volunteering to fetch the book your friend left behind in the car. As you work with your hands on the slightest of tasks, it helps you to stay sensitively connected to your physical environment. This contact is reassuring for your spirit. It also raises your aesthetic quotient—your quest for beauty in all situations. Moreover, when others see you connect with care and humility to your environment, they too are stimulated to do the same. I have tried that tray-sorting-exercise-in-flight a few times and every one who watches me immediately follows suit. That's news you can use!

I know a family that cleans the house together. They say it helps them appreciate one another, work away their stresses, bond over tasks, forget their complaints, de-clutter their minds, and enjoy much more whatever they have. A spiritual lady once remarked in a TV interview that when there is least traffic on the roads, like on a holiday, you could see the real landscape of your city. Likewise, when you clear up your field for vision, the superficial traffic ceases and you can behold your deeper priorities that were hidden behind the mess.

A neater physical space helps you think better. I remember the desk-cleaning ritual of my schooldays—clearing the table, placing stationary and books in neat piles before sitting down to prepare for that big math exam. Even now, all of us do a similar stocktaking of our things, clothes, accessories et al before appearing for an important interview or meeting. In fact, routine cleaning and renovation mark most festivities and rituals. Interestingly, the word in Hindi for festival is "Ut-sav," which means rising above your miseries. So apparently, you resort to clearing your outer messiness (as part of periodic festivities) to constantly make way for fresh and revitalizing energies. As you initiate activities to clear up your outer and inner mess, you become readier to, as an Indian guru says, "audit yourself, edit yourself."[33] Edit yourself playfully and it won't seem such a painful affair!

A note of caution, though: if you are a clean-freak a la Monica of *Friends* (I know many, including myself many years ago!), this very sorting of space can lead to more stress! For over-focused folks and perfectionists, what needs to be emphasized is the mindfulness and fun aspect of visual activities. So absorb yourself in activities. Suspend your judgments and controls and let yourself be led by something other than yourself. Working with soothing media like clay or working in natural spaces like gardens or listening to calming music during activity or consciously delegating tasks to others (allowing someone else to decide) can help control freaks to let go and resist their compulsive urge to always do things their way.

"Sorrow is the mere rust of the soul. Activity will cleanse and brighten it,"[34] said poet Samuel Johnson. You may have noticed that if you are going through an emotionally turbulent time in your life, being involved in some hands-on activity or project keeps your depression at bay and keeps your mind channeled toward a constructive goal. You avoid feeling bitter about your breakup or betrayal and fuel your confidence through achieving tasks. Likewise, for geriatrics, it is generally seen that the ones who keep themselves actively involved in day-to-day tasks like, looking after their plants or caring for their grandchildren, end up being more fulfilled and have least complaints about loneliness.

So when upset, don't reach out for the phone to sort out matters. Use the alibi of your space to subsume your stress. Remind yourself that any talk or exchange in your hyper state will go where it usually does—nowhere! Just as you wouldn't schedule a sales pitch to an important client after a hangover, likewise, avoid expression and exchange when you are hurt or upset. Expressing in the state of your emotional frenzy will lead to further bickering and blaming—more jabs, more scars, more complications. Turn to your visual playground for succor. Express yourself here and allow colors and shapes to bring release and order to your inner world.

Your hands serve your head as much as they serve your heart. "The hand is the cutting edge of the mind,"[35] said author and mathematician, Jacob Bronowski. Hands-on involvement in creative activities will simultaneously stimulate new learning and positive associations, engendering greater self-confidence. So in a few years, let's say the phrase 'crisis' may not just elicit feelings of loss or pain but equally those of inner strength and courage, which you tapped into given your positive processing of the negative stimuli. New experiences and new associations also mean that your brain is working behind the scenes to generate new neural connections. This activity, called neuro-genesis, is in fact a most potent and lasting anti-depression tonic.[36] So your hands cure you of your hurts and heartaches and energize your brain and imagination. You see more to life.

Manipulation of objects by children is known to be crucial for developing "creative thinking, or inventiveness."[37] The motor activity of your hands helps you to handle objects, and thus "handle ideas,"[38] as, says R. Arnheim. Author and innovator David Pensak believes that finding "multiple uses for just about every material you encounter"[39] will foster your innovative spirit. So take innovative liberties with objects. Invert their ordinary usage. Use a glass as a vase or a bench as a table. Move around things to suit alternative needs. Pull your chair from its regular place to a new angle. Or seat yourself in a different place in the conference room or lecture hall. In a new place, you will stay more alert; the way you are when you are in a foreign country.

Find things to do on smaller and bigger scales. Through doing, you beget direction. You boost your capacity to choose and decide. Doing also fosters daring. Doing makes you familiar with a terrain and familiarity makes you explore and take liberties in a positive way. As a result, you have more confidence and insight to deal with the challenges. And so makes you enjoy dealing with them.

Eventually, effortlessness in any domain is a result of effort. A study for found that musicians who practiced recorded less brain activity than those who were novices.[40] The findings are true of any task. Even in the kitchen, when kids helping mum are struggling to make a dessert, mum would have cooked a dinner for ten by then! Those who work harder can't help but get better.

Finally, as author and neurologist, Frank Wilson adds: "When personal discovery and desire prompt anyone to learn to do something well with the hands, an extremely complicated process is initiated that endows work with a powerful emotional charge. People are changed, significantly and irreversibly it seems, when movement, thought, and feeling fuse during the active, long term pursuit of personal goals." [41]

So do more and talk less!

A POSITIVE VISION OF YOUR LIFE

Create a nurturing visual environment in your homes and workplaces to help you to stay in a good mood and positive frame of mind. Have concrete goals to attend to. You will hardly have the time to talk or think against anyone when you have so much to do for something. Our next chapter shares stories of people whose involvement with the material realm helped them regain their confidence, balance their energies and feel buoyed by positive purposes.

Take the first step in faith. You don't have to see the whole staircase, just take the first step.
—Martin Luther King, Jr.

CHAPTER 2
PUTTING YOUR VISUAL SPHERE TO USE

To develop sensible subjective thinking, exercise your mind in the objective physical environment. With small steps in this sphere, you will take big strides in thinking in balanced and objective ways. In doing things with involvement, you will engage your creative ability to propose and achieve. You will also realize that to create fruitfully, you need to think objectively, from a variety of angles, and cannot just think in ways that suit your convenience or caprice.

Let's look at some cases where the uplifting influence of the visual realm helped people emerge from their depressive cocoon or insular understanding and balance their feelings and outlooks. I take the liberty of changing names and references and also coalescing different cases so as to give you a coherent and concise picture of different possibilities.

HEALING TRAUMA

Anita, a petite, shy nineteen-year-old Nepalese immigrant, worked at a small shop in a crowded bazaar in Delhi. Barely out of her teens, Anita was already a mother, an unwed one—a social stigma in the culture she came from, and even in the milieu where she sought refuge. Ayan, her son, was born to her as a result of rape by none other than her sister's husband. In order to protect the family honor and save the elder daughter's marriage, the family packed a pregnant Anita off to distant relatives in India. For the family, the matter was over. But Anita's ordeal had just begun.

The relatives weren't willing to look after her. Anita was soon left to fend for herself and her son in a foreign land and without an education or any particular skills for a job. But with a reference from a kind lady, she got employed as a shop-floor assistant in a mall, which gave her the means to take up an inexpensive tenement on rent in the neighborhood slum; not an easy place for a single mother. When I first met her in the mall, she looked weighed down by her circumstances. She smiled rarely, had a sunken look, and had a small, almost sad, voice.

I invited Anita and her son for play and picnic on her off day. Hoping to elicit Anita's *joie de vivre,* or at least her son's, I'd created a play site with assorted objects such as ribbons, twigs, pebbles, and wet clay. This colorful break in her dreary life seemed to enjoin her inner child. She began tinkering with the appealing assortment. She was attracted most to the wet clay in the large pot. She reached for it. In the hot Indian summer, that was surely a cool refuge! Anita probably took to clay because of its pliant nature—the only place where she would get a little sense of control over her life that seemed so much out of hand. Clay was responsive to her moves. It made her feel loved and worthy. Clay is also benevolent. It allows you to re-mould and redo your effort, accepting your mistakes with love. Interesting, "mud" is the root from which "mother" is derived![42]

In due course, Anita became more involved with her clay creations. Looking at them, she was assured of her ability to create and achieve in her own way. As Anita's confidence levels improved, she became more communicative. Her soft, weightless voices got a grain of gravity. Today, she runs her small enterprise of making and selling clay pots. Ayan goes to play school. His favorite activity is to throw the pots on the floor, which Anita painstakingly makes! Our children are our levelers!

What do you think would have happened if Anita had straightaway been involved in body-based work, facing pressures to perform and prove herself—for that too is a creative approach to improving confidence and having a healthy ego? In her case, it might have proved counterproductive. She had an uncomfortable relationship with her own body to begin with. It had brought her, as she perceived, stigma and separation from her family. Perhaps in another case, an alternate approach could have been more useful. All of us have different natures, different ways of responding, and different ways of coping.[43] So each case has to be looked at individually.

MANAGING ADOLESCENT STUBBORNNESS

Maya and Tara, siblings in their teens, would turn up their noses each time their mother suggested they take cooking class as summer courses. To the girls, exposed to the world of showbiz and glamour, cooking sounded like a most boring way to spend their summer holidays. But their mother reasoned that cooking skills would add great value to the girls' profiles when they eventually got married. The girls joked that in that case their mom should make them join belly dancing classes as one way or the other, the way to a man's heart was through the stomach! However, even as the jokes trailed off, the standoff prevailed. I was called in as a friend to sort out the matter.

Earlier their rapport was at stake. Now mine with them was as well! If I dared pander to either, I'd become an unwelcome guest in any case. I had to be tactful. In this moment of pressure, I recalled what a friend who often arbitrates in family matters had told me. He'd said that a balance in a dispute is struck best when both parties are equally unhappy and not when they are equally happy, for that can never be!

The mantra helped. I took away a bit from the goals of both parties and created a third goalpost—organizing a dance party, where the teenagers would cook and the parents would dance! Even though there were still differences and doubts, I at least got both parties to look in the same direction. The unhappiness of giving up a bit of their ideas was compensated well enough by the excitement generated for the new event. So now we were headed somewhere.

This more inclusive goal enabled both parties to dissolve opposition and turn collaborators. They had no choice! The work was divided. The girls wanted to organize the décor and music. They thoughtfully chose visual themes and musical numbers that would resonate with their parents' generation. Mom was the kitchen-queen and Dad was to keep a check on the accounts! The friends of the girls were to be recruited for service. The process of the organizing the party created many opportunities where differences had to be amicably resolved and optimal solutions favored over individual whims. During the event, all had a great time. After the event, they had detailed discussions over what all areas went right and what others suffered due to oversight. Importantly, they all relished their togetherness. They'd all worked as a team and materialized something they wouldn't have had they continued to look in different directions. To collaborate and experience this greater connection, all it takes is a bit of accommodation from your end. If you want something or someone to come into your life, you need to make room!

THE INDIVIDUALIST— LEARNING THE
REALITY OF INTERDEPENDENCE

This young woman was very talented but wouldn't mix with other people. She was good dancer and had read vastly. But having spent all time by herself, she had become intolerant of criticism and would escape all interpersonal contact. Her mother shared this problem with me, and requested that I counsel her. However, instead of talking to her about the value of cooperation, I thought it was better to put her in a situation where she would realize it on her own. Experiential learning is a powerful way to bring about a change of opinion and heart. I asked her if she was interested in being on the organizing committee of a global conference. As she was intellectually stimulated, she agreed immediately. To make the most of the opportunity, I dumped on her a lot more responsibility (than due!). I left her little option to work alone. She was put into tasks where she needed to ask for help. And she hadn't ever done that! My advantage was that she really wanted to be part of the program in a meaningful way. And when we have a degree passion, we are ready for a lot of quantum leaps.

I gave her the contact of other young people who were also part of the organizing group, should she need them for any help. She didn't look too keen. I wasn't surprised!

However, as expected (or set up!), she found herself ill equipped to handle things alone. She needed to reach out. She hesitantly contacted one person on the list and hesitantly asked for help. Of course, the other person responded positively as all had a shared goal. Gradually, she learnt of the contribution others were making and realized that her contribution was a mere drop in the ocean. That reality sobered her ego further and made her also value the work of others. She gradually came across many youngsters who were as talented as her, if not more.

Well, the positive environment worked its magic, and she began to blend in. She especially warmed up to the group as the seminar neared. They all would spend more hours, even after working schedule. An atmosphere of laughter and bonhomie reigned most of the time, except the occasional competitiveness to outperform the other. Competitive energies can however make you work harder and achieve more if you choose to get inspired by your competitor instead of becoming envious of him or her.

In our case, this girl's key competitor became her life-long collaborator— they fell in love! She looks much happier now. I guess that's all the therapy she needed—a satisfying bond.

CHANNELING AGGRESSION IN TEENS

Lack of love in our lives can make us aloof, or aggressive. At times, bullying, swearing, shouting, tantrums, and other symptoms of aggression could be purely defensive behavior—to mask an inner vulnerability, or the fear of getting hurt. In the case of this African girl diagnosed with Oppositional Defiant Disorder, the reasons stemmed from a troubled childhood. She'd moved through ten different foster homes by the age of sixteen. Her aggressiveness was not a form of arrogance but a mask to scare others and defend herself.[44]

A therapist in Russia using clay with visually impaired children likewise notes that most of these children release their angst and anxiety by pounding clay in aggressive ways.[45] That's probably because clay is too soft a target. If they'd try hitting metal, they'll soon learn that it hits back! Anyway, the point is that to handle aggression, you need to look beneath the boiling surface. Only then can you calm it in a sustainable way.

Challenge aggressive children by giving them hard targets. Their strong emotions and expressive force are a great opportunity to generate focus and get them into mission-mode over a constructive goal. For instance, you could ask them to make a large-sized collage with a variety of pictures pertaining to a current topic. When you provide a theme, you already provide a sense of direction. Physical and mental energies become less random and more purposeful. A collage also offers both the comfort of repetitious activity, such as cutting, placing, pasting, coloring, as well as the stimulation that comes with figuring out color, composition, and content. It also builds their sense of balance, proportion, and symmetry ... and in doing so tacitly build their sense of reasonableness, fairness, and controlled expression.

It would also help the teenagers to establish a healthy sense of self, as they uncover their own opinions, and mark their own likes and dislikes. For example, a theme such as: pick out ten pictures and articles from newspapers and magazines that you find disturbing and another ten that give you joy. This would greatly aid teens, their parents, and teachers in knowing their wards better. And with this insight, they can become proactive in molding their strengths.

Tools and materials like crayons, markers, scissors, adhesives, glitter-pens, glow-stickers, colored wires, bits of colored paper, or fabrics would make this learning activity a lot of play and fun. To remind them of their achievements—and all the hard work and resourcefulness they are capable of—photograph (even autograph!) their favorite creations and create some applied art with it. Make wall hangings, transpose on a coffee mug, and get it stamped as watermark on a T-shirt or pasted on a book cover. Encourage them to move on instead of resting on past laurels. This kind of activity also works well with obese teens (or adults as well) that have an undying urge to keep eating all the time. It diverts their attention to other pastures, more fulfilling ones.

For over-stimulated teens, you need a bigger setting and stage. I know of a group of students in a college who were always creating trouble for others. A counselor involved them into painting these colossal machines dumped in the college backyard. Today, the boys are proud of the product of their labor. They even got a prize for their work, whereas just a few months ago they were penalized for ruining property!

Sometimes when the weight of emotions is too heavy too bear, like when you lose a dear one, again taking on a gigantic work of dedication to this one's memory can heal you. So do something that you imagine will give peace to that soul. You can't fill the void but you can always create a better memory of it. And in doing so, emerge stronger from the loss.

MASK—EXPLORING YOUR EXPRESSIONS

Masks can help you identify your aspirations or express your hidden feelings. Masks bare our emotions in black and white. There isn't much ambiguity in a mask. The face on a mask clearly projects emotions like kindness, wickedness, jealousy, arrogance, vanity, and power. What kind of masks do you feel comfortable in? Which ones do you like to play with and explore? Which ones do you avoid? Likewise, which roles do you like to play and which others do you avoid? Do some roles make you feel more comfortable, or more powerful, or more sincere? Keenly observe your own behavior in different contexts to see when certain masked energies become more manifest.

A girl I knew had a dominating demeanor in her interactions. But when it came to choosing masks, she would also go for the ones that had a soft and kind look. There seemed to be a disconnection between her suggested and subconscious needs. Did she want to control others through her aggressive behavior or did she want to feel secure and loved? We began a dialogue on what she really wanted.

I interrogated her from a variety of standpoints to help her uncover and discover her real needs and motives. In her case, it turned out that she'd always wanted the men in her family to protect her, but they would always leave her to fend for herself. She learned to hide her vulnerable side in her real life, but the guise of the mask allowed her to access it again.

She had the good sense to accept this deeper truth and not defiantly hold on to her protective veneer. She now uses creative visualizations to release her fears and has become more natural in her behavior.

NATURE—THE CURE-ALL

Nature is a natural calmer for all. It has something for everybody. The sheer project size of nature is humbling, let alone her inventiveness and immaculate design at every possible level.

If you want to compete with someone, let that one muse be nature! You'll be inspired and humbled at the same time. However, competition with nature will eventually turn into collaboration, because you can't compete with your caretaker! That is the crucial lesson of working with your environment—you need to work in harmony with it.

So treat your environmental resources as your family inheritance. Nature's abundance is all there for you. Respect it and allow it to nurture you even more. Trust in nature's intelligence. It has always served you. It made sure that you evolved in the womb and out of it. It will ensure that you progress even now.

Make it your partner and feel connected to it. Develop a rapport with nature, a sort of vital connection, the way you feel with your family and friends. Spend time in it. Reflect on its creative prowess.

Look out for the miraculous in the mundane. The other day while walking, I observed that baby plants were enjoying the support of tall sticks. Now, they wouldn't be blown away by the slightest breeze and would grow tall despite the rough weather. This observation of natural and commonsensical phenomena triggered a deeper reflection. I wondered if such a support is available to us. And the answer I found was that yes, indeed, if we can hold on faithfully to the idea that nature will nurture us, no matter what, then that firm belief will act like the tall, unbending stick and make us attain our heights despite the odds.

KNOW YOURSELF TO NURTURE YOURSELF

As you start doing more, you will learn of your strengths and weaknesses. This is the exciting moment of your personal journey— where your outer material is stimulating you to express and articulate all that is within you, including unprocessed feelings and fears and unquestioned beliefs. Involvement in the visual realm will help you differentiate between dreams and delusions. It will make you see the prejudices that are mixed up with your priorities. It will enable your greater witnessing and through it a conscious approach to seeing and feeling. You will choose ways that soothe your nerves, strengthen your spirit, and boost your balanced thinking. Your creative vision will thus unfold.

A vision is not just a picture of what could be; it is an appeal to our better selves, a call to become something more.
—Rosabeth Moss Kant

CHAPTER 3

CREATIVE VISION —
ENERGIZE YOUR IMAGINATION

I n the Oscar-winning movie *Slumdog Millionaire* (2009), there is a lot you can choose to see: poverty, crime, exploitation, apathy… A friend in America, who is also a screenwriter, asked me about my response to the film. I found myself saying: *It's a film about keeping innocence and integrity in your heart despite the odds. If the protagonist could be preoccupied with love, despite his most challenging circumstances, so can most of us. A French writer once said that going to India will cure anyone's depression … I hope this film about India will stimulate many people to see all that they have in their lives, over and above what they do not.*

We see what speaks to us. Have you noticed that when you buy a cherry (or any) colored car, you start spotting so many cherry colored cars on the road from then! Well, they were always there. You just see them more because the color now means something more to you. Likewise, if you believe in love more than others, you will see it more than them. If you are prone to self-pity, you will perceive an insult where others wouldn't. If you are overconfident, you will hear and see a gushing compliment where none was intended. In a similar vein,

Milan Kundera says in his novel, *Ignorance*, *"People who see their lives as a shipwreck set out to hunt down the guilty parties."*

The more dominant trait in your makes you see and hear the way you do. However, different roles or energies predominate in different relationships. So if a guest accidentally drops hot coffee on your carpet, you will be less forgiving even if more polite. But if your child does the same, you will be more concerned about his or her well-being than that of the carpet. In the first case, the spot on the carpet will create prejudice vis-à-vis the guest. In the second case, your heart will make you process your feelings with due prioritization and make you seek solutions for the carpet without prejudice and with objectivity.

So where your heart is determines the kind of calculations your head does. In order to inspire your head, just place the heart in a good spot! Or train your imagination to see and feel sunshine in all kinds of weather.

I present some strategies!

VISION THROUGH OUTLOOK: SEEK BALANCED AND ENERGIZING VIEWS

Even if you can't change your setting, you can always change your seat! Just like you scout for a seat in a theater that provides optimal view, make a similar effort in your life to choose stances that make you feel better about your situation. Even if you feel bad for a moment, you've got to quickly look out for some good news in the bad news.

A good strategy to awaken such positive orientations is to focus on your advantages and discount your limitations. Simply put, embrace what you have and endure what you don't. You will become much more lighthearted vis-à-vis your problems and also unleash their positive potential through your generous participation. I once met a group of students visiting India who would clap whenever there would be a power outage and would be gleeful at the new opportunity of having a 'candle-lit' dinner instead! They could have whined and complained, but they chose to enjoy the moment for what it was. That is because they were positively predisposed to enjoy their adventure in India. That positive stance made them see everything as part of their experience and discovery; including those issues that could have seemed problematic even to Indians!

Another strategy to appreciate your own life is to displace yourself from your familiar context and try out a new one. An example concerns this teenager who was eternally dissatisfied with her life. She could never see what all she had. So her parents thought of a good way to make her see it! They packed her off to a summer school organized by an orphanage. There, she met children who didn't have parents or a home to call their own. She came home rather sobered down and told her parents: "Actually, my problems are not as critical as I once thought they were." Yours aren't either!

To sustain your positive outlooks, develop gratitude and latitude in your thinking. Reflect upon your great resources. Imagine your life sans your parents, house, body, food, water, computer, friends, car et al. Feel the loss. All that you take for granted will then look like gains. Take the fabled story of this businessman who lost all his savings and wealth and thus said life was not worth living anymore. God appeared before him and said, "If I return all your wealth to you, what will you give in return?"

"Anything you ask for," he said promptly.

So, God asked for his head. Of course he was not going to give that. So God asked for his eyes, then ears, then nose, then tongue, then hands, then legs… The businessman wasn't willing to give any. In the end the businessman says, "God, I really think I have a lot already. I don't want the money back. I will earn it on my own!"

I once heard of a man paralyzed from the neck down who pushed the numbers on his cell phone with his nose. That made be thankful for my fingers and also imagine what life would be without them. So there are many of these stories all around us that can help reduce our obsessive picking on our problems and see our life with a positive outlook. I once met students at MIT who were part of a project to live on less that $2 a day. They told me how much this experience made them understand a poor man's plight and also count their blessings. So if you are worried about lack of money, you too can spend a day with people who work eighteen hours a day and earn in a month what you spend in a day.

Make a collage of such stories. Browse through them often. They will make you feel fortunate and free you from false annoyances. So if you are irritated at the fact that there is no soda to accompany your meal today, turn to your humble glass of water with eyes of appreciation. Remind yourself of thousands in the desert who walk miles and then line up for hours in the scorching sun to be able to fetch a pitcher of water for their parching children. Your glass of water will look ambrosial.

Interestingly, when you begin to value what you have, you add value to it. An American lady told me that to cope with the period of recession, she turned for succor to her family and relationships. She began to appreciate her loved ones more. As a result, the family became a much more closely-knit unit. Neglect of what we have can negate its force, whereas appreciating whatever little we have can magnify its energy.

You can energize your outlooks, even in tough situations, by seeing the universe with trust and faith. Look at this story. A businessman has a windfall gain of a million dollars in a deal. When asked how he feels about it, he said, "The going is good." In a few months, the same businessman lost some millions in another event. When asked how he felt about it, he again says, "The going is good." People wonder how the going can be good in both cases! Shouldn't he have been really happy in the first case and sad in the second? Ordinarily, that would be our predicament!

But unlike us, this businessman had adopted an energizing outlook to save himself from stresses and stay calm and centered in both ups and downs. His saw himself as a caretaker of this enterprise and not as its owner. He said that god was the real owner. And so his job on the ground was to do his best to maintain the well-being of his company and solve problems with a cool mind. So he treated all ups and downs as a matter of 'news' that he had to take stock of in order to respond effectively to the challenges ahead. This view of himself as No. 2 in the power hierarchy (even though he was number one) prevented his overreactions. His job was to keep things good, whatever turn situations take.

If this person can do it, so can we. If you really want to stay positive, nothing can make you negative. But you must take the help of some energizing outlooks. So if you have a strict mother, start seeing her as a teacher of patience. If you have a competitive colleague, look upon him as someone who is there to push you to work harder. It doesn't matter what others are giving to you. What matters more is what you are receiving.

However, despite your best attempts to stay upbeat about what you have, you will at times (many times!) feel sorry for yourself or feel ashamed for having overreacted or feel angry with others for taking advantage of you. In the grip of negative thinking, you will spoil your mood and mull over all that is wrong with others and your life. You need to get out of here!

Regain your balance through invoking inner silence and witnessing your negative thoughts. Just like gripping a pillar in a moving bus helps you to keep your balance despite the bumps, in the same way clinging to your inner silence will prevent you from succumbing to the inexorable pull of negative energies. In the film *A Beautiful Mind*, the protagonist is overtaken by hallucinations. But he overcomes his mistaken thinking by recognizing the fact that his mind is playing tricks on him. He sees the monsters coming but he does not open the doors of his imagination to them. You need to do the same.

So the way out of a down is simply accept that you are going through a depressive phase. That awareness will distance you from your negative thoughts and prevent you from exciting them through your emotional reactions. So basically, you will avoid fanning the fire of pain and generating the smoke of suffering. In due course, the inner flames will die down. So when you slip into a negative state every now and then, become silent to curtail its force.

Just remember that worrying or losing heart will only weaken your spirit. Now, would you invest in an activity that leads to depreciation of your money? Of course not! So why invest in thoughts that negate the courage of your spirit! Instead, enjoy the fact that your brain has a developed capacity to spot many factors at play in your environment. Your acute observation of your environment can help you visualize how things could turn out to be, and that can help you make vigilant choices. Therefore, avoid reacting to facts. Absorb them instead.

Moreover, when you discover problems in some situation, recognize them but do not focus beyond on them. When you start affirming problems, they cloud your vision and bring down your motivation and cheer. Play this simple exercise with a friend: show her a picture of a scenic mountain area with a house and tell her not look out for the broken window glass pane. She will most certainly notice that all throughout!

In fact, if you meditate on problems, you will soon start imagining problems where none exist! Such a negative state of mind will make you find faults with everything and everyone. And you constant carping will fulfill your negative prophesy as well.

It is far more worthwhile to make your positive thoughts come true. Even if they are fancies today, they can become realities tomorrow. But you've got to commit yourself to them. You've got to start believing in them. You've got to start visualizing them. So let's see how convert the virtual into the visual!

VISION THROUGH VISUALIZATION: LOOK ELSEWHERE OR OTHERWISE!

What you see as a reality today must have begun as a dream somewhere. Persistent pursuit of our dreams is what turns them into realities, no matter how fanciful they seem to others.

Visualizing a picture in your mind is the beginning toward creating it. Interestingly, actually something or visualizing it means the same kind of activity for your brain, as it recruits the same visual regions in both cases.[46] Research (2008) also suggests "that imagining something changes vision both while you are imagining it and later on."[47]

But indeed, seeing something physical and real is easier to believe in and get energized by as compared to seeing something in your mind. Visualizing an unseen reality that you hope will materialize sometime in the future requires much more conviction and motivation on your part. Yet, if you can do this hard work, it will leave you with a stronger ability to create realities after your own vision. It will pave the way for your independent thinking and action.

You can use visualizations for a variety of purposes. You can ease anxiety through relaxing visualizations. It's been proven that to relax your brain in less than thirty seconds, all you need to do is close your eyes and visualize a peaceful picture![48] Pregnant women use this to good effect to remain calm during delivery. You can use them to transform negative images/feelings into positive ones. Perhaps you saw a terrible accident or an image from a horror movie that continues to make you fearful. Or perhaps you feel shameful of something you did to another, or angry with what someone did to you. You can neutralize such negative feelings through suitable visualizations that usher in hope, forgiveness and transformation.

So let's say, to let go of your malice, you can visualize your anger as a black spot and forgiveness as a bright golden light. Imagine that this golden light replacing the black spot. You can also use do a visual ritual. Like this friend once told me that she invested all her confusions, questions, anger, and anxiety in a stone. She held it tight spoke to it and asked it to carry away all her negative emotions. She then dropped this stone into the flowing river; a symbolic way of releasing her inner toxicity into embrace of the motherly universe. Now we all tend to hold on to thoughts and feelings. So visualize for letting go.

Look at it this way: when flying a kite, if you don't let go, the kite won't soar in new directions. Letting go helps you to grow (while holding on secures you). In fact, even in businesses, where one would think that you need to hold on to money to become successful, the key to growing is in letting go! In a conference, a delegate asked a senior venture capitalist about the attitudes that enable a business leader to grow from strength to strength. And the panelist just suggested one thing—cultivate the capacity to delegate and let go. Letting go is not about giving up on life. It's about getting more from it.

You can also visualize for healing physical illnesses. If you or a dear one is suffering from let's say a stone in kidney or a tumor in some part, visualize that the illness is going away and health is restored. A doctor told me that many cancer cases were heading for remission as a result of this video game that urged them to fight their malignant cells and replace them with healthy ones. Healing and transformation begin in your mind indeed. And your mind is rather responsive to visuals and rituals.

Always visualize for a positive purpose. If you visualize that your rival is losing money or your classmate is getting lower grades, the pictures won't do much for your well-being or progress. And if your rival still gets better grades, you'll become all the more bitter and lose your confidence. What's the point! It is much more useful to see yourself going up instead of seeing others coming down. And you need to know that there's room for many on the top. Life is not like a pyramid where there is room for just a few on the top and you need to jostle for space. Life is a sphere that keeps expanding as you expand. The space is endless. So don't narrow your horizons. If you some problem is shrinking your imagination, visualize to let go of it!

When you can visualize with ease the kind of pictures you want, you will become your own mood-swing manager! You will be able to find beauty in the banal with just some twists and turns of your imagination.

Visualizations can help you prepare your mind for various eventualities. So use your poetic license to create scenarios. Imagine how you are likely to act in response to different situations. Improve your responses now that you have the time.

You can visualize your worst fears and make your peace with them. Just don't panic when you are visualizing! For just like a surgeon can only operate on a patient when he or she is calm and still, in the same way visualization will only enable your thinking if you stay relaxed. To continue, take for example that you are really nervous about your college admissions. You really want to get into this famous one but you aren't sure if you will. And that uncertainty is making you anxious. So to allay your fears of not getting admission to your favorite college, look at this possibility in the eye. Accept such a scenario in your mind. This isn't about losing hope or becoming negative. It's about freeing your mind. As you accept this situation as a possibility, you will end up putting your best, and not anxious, foot forward while writing your essays and appearing for your interviews. Now that kind of performance is likely to get you admission! And even if it doesn't, you're mentally prepared for plan B!

Sometimes visualizing the worst outcome can be painful, like when a dear one is unwell or hospitalized. In that case, simply pray for a positive outcome. Pray with faith. Just like words ring true when backed by feelings, wishes come true when backed by faith.

A lot of us, initially, have huge troubles visualizing clearly (and even relaxing fully!). However, the only way to become better at it is to keep at it! Even passive and hazy visualization will in due course lead you to greater concentration and clarity.[49] To enhance your concentration, you can use the yogic exercise of staring at an object or at a lit lamp. To add weight to the visuals, use props. In many relaxation techniques, a normal instruction is to imagine a sandbag on your body, or even using a real one, to help you surrender your body to the lap of mother earth. Then you know what to feel!

Visualize your dreams as concrete goals. An image will make your invisible dream look real and attainable. Follow up on it with hard work. Whenever self-doubt creeps in, visualize again. This book too started in mind as a visual. I saw it ready in my mind much before I wrote it! It's a bit like what happens when you declare your plans to the world. Then you have to live up to them!

Use visualization to get your larger purpose of a stress-free, happy life firmly etched in your consciousness. Create a picture that helps you in perspective taking whenever you are getting overwhelmed by day-to-day pressures. A successful businessman uses a space-stellar visualization to help him de-stress and take due distance from daily problems so that they do not throw him off-balance. So just before being driven to a crucial meeting, he pictures himself floating weightlessly and serenely in outer space, crossing hundreds and thousands of stars and suns. From that large outer space, he sees the earth as a small speck and voila, his daily struggles don't appear so magnified at all. The big noises in his head soften down to distant whisperings. His head gets lighter, his spirits soar as he places all the movement in his mind and life in due perspective.

An e-mail forward doing the rounds these days tells you to look at a picture of where the Earth in relation to the solar system, and then in to the many galaxies. It appears smaller than a speck of sand, if it hasn't utterly disappeared by then! This larger view helps to correct our false perception that we are the center of the world. So if you are upset with your friend just because he or she forgot your birthday, then take the larger view to see all those other people in your life who have never wished you on your birthday, or those who do not even know the date or year of their birth. The broader vision corrects our narrow thinking and releases us from negative feelings.

Finally, with positive thinking, you will be able to see the many factors at play in your relationships and environment without getting hassled. This state of mind is ideal to make use of all the data!

VISION THROUGH INVOLVEMENT:
SEE MANY FACTORS AT PLAY

You need to take a close look at life to take a good look at it. You need hands-on involvement in the playground of real life to know how things really work. Only then can you make them work better through your strategic intervention.

Developing a keen observation is the first step toward improved understanding of your environment. Sharpen your visual observation by stopping to look at things that you would normally ignore. For instance, in your office, notice the length and shape of the boundary wall. Or investigate the windows to see how they work. Look around. Be curious. Ask questions.

Author R. Arnheim notes that when you are deprived of visual and acoustic stimulation, viz. given nothing but "diffuse light for the eyes and a steady buzz for the ears,"[50] you can't think right. However, in our daily lives, the problem is not so much of lack of stimulation, but absence of an aware rapport with our physical realities. We normally become so mechanical in our routines that we miss seeing the obvious. Our world then passes us by instead of informing us.

The second benefit of involvement is that it leads us to look at real problems and solve them for what they are. In fact, when your mind doesn't have enough real images and pictures (gathered through your greater observation), your brain begins to imagine all sorts of unreal things and harbors illusions.[51] For example, when you are directly involved in organizing a dinner, your mind will go over real issues like who to invite, what menu to offer, how to serve etc. However, if your spouse is also participating in the organization, albeit indirectly (giving armchair guidance!), he or she is likely to issue instructions that can be whimsical. I am sure you've been through moments when you had to say this to your spouse, "Why don't you do this yourself and see what I am going through!"

The third benefit of hands-on and real time involvement is that since the buck stops at your table, you push your inventiveness to find solutions. You use commonsensical and natural approaches to handle pressures. So rehearse enough in the playfield of life. Volunteer, participate, and collaborate in family events and community projects.

The fourth benefit of sustained involvement is efficiency and ease you gain from your repeated exposure and long-term engagement with a given field. Notice the efficiency with which your mom works in the kitchen and compare it to yours. Her involvement over many years gives her a greater capacity for multi-tasking and multidimensional thinking. She can mix things intuitively whereas you need to keep going back to your measuring jugs and recipe books!

Eventually, as a result of seeing many factors at play and your ability to mentally visualize the bigger picture, you will improve your envisioning prowess. Better envisioning will lead to better provisioning. So if you can envision the possibility of, let's say, a fire during festive celebrations, you are more likely to have a strategy in place for coping with a possible fire break out. You'll equip yourself with a fire extinguisher, ask people to wear cottons and avoid nylons, and communicate to others the emergency plans. It is, of course, a possibility that the fire may never ever happen. Or that it may happen in a way that you didn't imagine at all. However, your prior mental preparation will help you to act in the moment with greater presence of mind.

On the route of involvement, you need to know how to make sense of your trials and errors. For you only discover better ways of doing by making your fair share of mistakes. There is this anecdote in business circles on how a manager who has an impeccable record of no mistakes needs to get fired!

David Pensak, innovator and global speaker, says that for innovation to occur mistakes should be not just indulgently tolerated but actively rewarded![52] Likewise, Professor Dennett at Tufts University proposes, "You should seek out grand opportunities to make mistakes, just so you can recover from them."[53]

You thus need conscious and positive outlooks toward failure and errors. I'd say that instead of mulling over your mistakes, feeling guilty, or looking for scapegoats, just learn from them. Trying out a new way is better than not trying at all. And if someone makes you feel that you were really stupid, admit to him or her that you were! Put the debate to rest!

However, censure from our family members and stigma in society can discourage the best among us from trying out new ways. We therefore need a culture of respecting mistakes in our homes and society. To understand the positive impact of supportive attitudes, consider this: in the United States, where society is more accepting of trial and error, 10 percent of start-ups succeed. This might look meager compared to the fact that 70 percent of Indian start-ups succeed. However, the American appetite for risk encourages more people to try. Therefore, over a thousand people who try, even if 10 percent succeed, that still creates a hundred entrepreneurs! In India, given the society's negative view of failure, only a hundred will try as compared to the thousands in the US.

So support your dear ones when they fail or fall. Hold their hands and heal their hearts. No one feels good about failing. Why make them feel worse? Instead, use the opportunity of a loss to emerge stronger, together.

Mistakes are also precious learning curves because they bring home a moment of insight or realization. Your mistake-turned-into-realization transforms you. So you actually gain in wisdom if you allow yourself to positively relate to your error or loss. Author Richard Bach says in a similar spirit: "*That's what learning is, after all: not whether we lose the game, but how we lose and how we've changed because of it, and what we take away from it that we never had before, to apply to other games. Losing, in a curious way, is winning.*"[54]

Of course, pre-empt mistakes through careful observation and evaluation too. Do your homework: reflect upon various possibilities, envisage your responses, and importantly invite the involvement and advice of people you trust. Two brains can see more than one. That's why perhaps Japanese companies negotiate with multi-member teams— because each member can see something, given his unique positioning and focus, which may be easily missed by another. Chinese companies likewise require senior managers to be involved with processes at the factory floor, so that the company gets a truer overall perspective. Understanding the many sides of a story is crucial for your just and justified vision.

However, take care not to lose the bigger picture in the zeal of involvement. You are working hard to reach somewhere. So don't forget 'where'! Take for example this company that was making beef burgers. The beef slices were large round pieces that were cut from square slabs. In the cutout a lot of good meat was being wasted, so the company decided to mince these wasted meat portions and offer them as a bowl of minced meatballs at very low prices, since their input cost was only the wasted meat. But unexpectedly, these low-cost minced meatballs caught the imagination of the consumer and became a huge success. Demand soared and soon outstripped supply. What did the company do? So excited were they with their success that they actually started mincing fresh slabs of meat to make the low-cost meatballs! Of course, they ran into huge losses. What went wrong? They simply lost sight of the larger picture of why they had introduced minced meatballs in the first place and why they had kept the prices low.

Likewise in life, sometimes in our excited involvement in the present, we lose perspective of the future. Like when you are partying with friends, don't you forget you have school at seven the morning after? But your mom doesn't! She is seeing what you aren't—the bigger picture. So the next time she calls to remind you that you need to be home, see her intervention with understanding.

The final benefit is that when you can see the larger picture, you can make intelligent interventions or smart moves to alter the dynamics of a situation. For instance, if you have a hyper-energetic adolescent son, and no amount of counseling is helping, use your sensitive and sharp assessment of all the factors at play. Maybe he doesn't have many friends, or maybe he doesn't have enough engaging or challenging hobbies, or maybe he is watching too much television. So instead of chastising him, simply change the rules of the game. In coping with the new situation, he will have to change his ways!

Seeing the bigger picture can also correct your judgmental behavior. The moment you see bigger, you think better. Take the instance of this lady from abroad that was peeved at the way zesty salesmen in Indian cities would pester her to buy their wares. We began discussing about their lives and I gave her a graphic picture of their backgrounds and typical struggles. She had a shift of perception. Instead of getting irritated with them, she now looked upon them as "simple people trying out to eke an honest living." Her whole outlook changed toward them and they all had a much more positive interaction.

Overall, your personal involvement equips you with a variety of facts. But you need your feelings in place to make sense of the facts!

VISION THROUGH EMPATHY: SEE OTHERS WITH A HEART

When our heart is involved, we respond to facts and situations in more accommodating ways. To take an instance, if your daughter were to add too much spice by mistake to some dishes for dinner, wouldn't you find ways to ease her problem instead of rubbing it in? You would simply tell her, "Don't worry honey. We'll just add some sugar!"

Now, imagine the same situation in your colleague's house. Given your emotional distance, you will be much less generous. You may not say anything rude but might make your discomfort evident to your colleague.

But you can address the facts here differently, through your empathy. Play a mind game to see your colleague as your daughter or sibling. This new image will press your heart into action. The heat of your heart melts away bad vibes and cold shoulders. As you warm up to the other in a spirit of fellow feeling, you will find yourself saying and doing things that help your colleague feel lighter, and not lousier. With this sweetness in place, you will now be able to enjoy the same dish that was annoying you just as while ago. Your colleague will be moved by your kindness. Wouldn't you be?

Bridge your sense of separation from others through your imagination. See your friends as family: you'll become more forgiving. Focus on your shared humanity: you will become much less judgmental. Replace some of your critical attitudes with a bit of concern. Your concern will move another's spirit and create new spaces of positive exchange.

See with empathy even during casual observation. I was once waiting in the queue at a city airport when I saw a frail old man with partial vision and unstable gait. He couldn't read, write or speak the native language, and was struggling to answer all sorts of questions at the security check. I began to wonder: where had he come from? What was he was doing here alone, without any family member around? Did he have enough money? Looking at him, I was also reminded of older people in my family. This imaginative bond of kinship moved me all the more. I began seeing him with kindness. I began sending him my prayers. I also reflected on my good health and education. I felt a surge of gratefulness. It slowed me down. It have me depth.

In your mind, record and replay such stirring moments of reflection. Replace your worry-time with empathy-time.

However, the idea is not to feel bad about life or situations. Emotions are your vital force. They make you think and act with feeling. Just channel them into purposes that speak to you. Turn them into your passions.

VISION THROUGH PASSION AND PURPOSE: SEE WHERE YOUR HEART IS!

In following your heartfelt purpose, you will find your potential.

The appeal of a personal purpose is so great that people often give up money for meaning. In the Hindi film, *Swades* (2004), the protagonist is a successful NRI (Non-Resident-Indian or Non-Returning-Indian, as the heroine quips!) working with NASA and has a promising career ahead. However, a chance engagement with his village and its inhabitants makes him aware of the many social, educational, and economic issues that are keeping them backward and hindering progress. After being part of a project of brining electricity to this village, during which he brings a fractured community together (and also finds his lady love), he realizes that his heart is truly here. When he contemplates leaving his American job (a dream for many in the village!), his friends and seniors advise him against it. But he listens to his heart and goes back to the village in order to play a role that seems more meaningful to him.

A sense of connection to our purpose drives our passion. And with passion, you will readily endure challenges and even use them to your advantage.

Yet, how will you become aware of a cause that is close to your heart? Sometimes a brief interaction with someone or your involvement with a situation can spark off a deeper quest. Laurie Baker, the British architect who created low-cost sustainable housing for the poor in India found heartfelt vision (and turned it into a life-long mission) just after a brief interaction with Mahatma Gandhi. Likewise, this MBA student began working on a college project of surveying the lives of pavement dwellers (homeless who live, not just sleep, on the city pavements). She was so moved by the end of it that it caused a shift in her aspirations— she now wants to use her education to make a difference to the lives of the homeless because that gives meaning to hers.

Yet, you need hard work and sustained pursuit to understand what truly matters to you, as also it's why and how. Professor J. S. Feinstein from Stanford says: "*Over time, as an individual thinks about his interest, reflects upon it, makes connections among different concepts, ideas, images, works, phenomena, facts, and other elements that fit with it, and imagines it more fully, he develops his interest conceptually, and it becomes clearer, more integrative and more coherent; ... he forms a fuller conception of it.*"[55]

Further, when you are clear in your mind and committed to your vision, you will naturally find optimal routes to deliver it. At an entrepreneurship conference in New Delhi, the vice president of an MNC remarked that to grow, any enterprise needs above all a keen and clear sense of purpose.[56] There is this oft-cited case study (even at Harvard) of an Indian organization that was driven to provide low-cost eye care to poor people. That inclusive purpose enabled it to configure a sustainable business model based on high volumes. An eye-operation costs less than $2 per person and the volumes ensure decent profits. So meaning is not at odds with money. In fact, money yields you more satisfaction when you use it for purposes that are meaningful to you.

To gather courage for your purpose and release its positive potential, you need to make room for the cosmic vision. Without it, anxiety might mount and you may be affected by ridicule or opposition. But your passion and purpose can one day be a veritable force of change and a harbinger of new realities. Therefore, you need to maintain your commitment to your invisible dreams—because one day they will become visible to the world. So keep safe that irrational drive to dream and dare. Energize it by developing a warm connection with the cosmic vision and placing your faith in it.

Now most of us have felt a mysterious play going on between our individual thoughts and cosmic plans. There are many situations where we find that man proposes and god superimposes. A man who was cursing his luck for missing his bus to office later realized his providential escape—he'd missed the bus to his office in WTC on the morning of 9/11. Likewise, an Indian minister escaped an assassination attempt thanks to the rats in the field that chewed away the cables that were meant for the blow-up.[57]

So there is something out there that is working for your well-being. It is willing to support your dreams. It is ready to guide you toward your purpose and help you give it form and shape. Recognize this player and give it the pride of place in your life. You will energize its contribution all the more. This faith will enable your courage to take risks and rise above the odds.

Now a nurse who was a key witness in the terror attacks in Mumbai in November 2008 was scared to testify in her individual capacity. But she found her courage to act from her conscience and rise above her fears when she wore her uniform. Indeed faith is that uniform that will immediately make you feel connected to your cosmic source and cover. You will feel as if you belong to it and you need to uphold its positive vision at all costs. Your sense of duty, your bigger purpose, your fearless thinking, and your veritable direction will all become evident with one stroke of faith.

FROM VISION TO ACTION

To take your dreams meaningfully into the world, you need help. You may have noticed that to sing in tone, you need to be accompanied by instruments and collaborators who are also in tone and in sync. Ergo, you too need to be enabled and upheld by your larger environment in order to successfully implement your dreams.

So you need ways to keep egos out of the way and bring more friendship and warmth into the picture. You need to nurture relationships through conscious attitudes and positive habits. In doing so, you will chance upon new dreams and new sources of energy.

The whole of next section is about tapping into the great creative potential of your interpersonal realm—the exciting theater of relationships.

PART II: BEING

Strengthening Your Relationships: Playing And Progressing In The Theater Of Life

"Ven. Ananda said to the Blessed One: "This is half of the holy life, lord: admirable friendship, admirable companionship, admirable camaraderie."

Buddha: "Don't say that, Ananda. Don't say that. Admirable friendship, admirable companionship, admirable camaraderie is actually the whole of the holy life."[1]

CHAPTER 4

WE RELATE, THEREFORE WE ARE

The theater of life can be rich, reassuring or rude. You can love it or lament it, but you can't leave it. It's actually an indispensable partner in the realization of your fuller self. Learning and growing in the theater of life can be great fun when you have constructive approaches to respond to the diversity of characters, situations, and egos! That is what this section will help you develop.

DIVERSITY: DEVELOPING YOU

Diversity makes the terrain of life uneven and chaotic. That is what perplexes us. But challenges and changes in your environment will not stress you if you are mentally prepared to accept them and meet them in a positive spirit. It is similar to when you embark knowingly on an adventure. You are then mentally prepared to encounter challenges and are always alert to the possibility of one around the corner. So you equip yourself in advance with suitable tools and attitudes to put your best foot forward in a situation. You are also quick to learn your lessons from bad choices or mistaken thinking and prepare yourself better for future adventures. You need to do the same for life. Accept the fact that life will indeed challenge you at every step of the way. (If it doesn't, you should feel ignored!) Recognize the fact that life wants you to evolve through whatever curriculum it puts forth for you. Trust the fact that life is trying its level best to help you find your fuller self, even if its means look strange!

Now, even in a yoga class, the instructor takes you through a range of unusual, sometimes impractical, and often unbalancing postures that seem to be a far cry from bringing you peace or silence. But then, when you've jumped like a crow, stretched like a dog, stood like a tree, puffed out like a cobra—basically, stretched yourself in every way and found your balance even in the most challenging positions— you feel much more in touch with your deeper capabilities. And that gives inner security and satisfaction.

Also, in struggling to cope with challenging postures, you find new coping skills. More exposure to problems and questions will improve your ability to respond. So you won't breakdown upon the slightest emotional overload. Then as you find multiple coping ways, you will enrich your inner repertoire of creative approaches. You will store the know-how of different tactics that work positively in different contexts. So your spirit will evolve into something like a Swiss knife—equipped with multipurpose tools to come to your aid in different situations. Equipped thus, you will not see challenges as obstacles or sources of stress, but just as problems that need to be solved. Just like solving problems in schools exams fetched you good marks and enabled your graduation to the next, so it will be in life too.

In fact, you now might even create challenges deliberately to evolve in spirit, just like sportspeople do in order to improve their physical endurance and performance. I once read of a family that actually made a house with uneven floors because they wanted to be challenged everyday into finding their balance! So if others tell you that you are crazy to experiment with life, tell them you aren't alone! Now our world is where it is today because of those who dared to go beyond. So try a new approach. Overcome your conditioning. Use your daily situations as sites of experimentation for your better ideas. You will discover your originality.

Look at it the positive contribution of diversity in another way. Isn't a situation of disagreements preferable to one where others are only telling you how good you are and how right your thought processes are? Then you'd actually become imprisoned in your image of yourself and develop an inflated ego. So let other punch holes in your thoughts! Allow the disagreements to chisel your spirit and nuance your understanding. Winning the argument will yield momentary pleasure. Reflecting upon it can change you forever.

So learn from your adverse situations and also your adversaries. Imbibe in yourself what you like in others and reject in yourself what you criticize in others. Have faith that all situations that come to pass are all blessings, or blessing-in-disguise. Respond to all challenges with calm and patience, no matter what the provocation. You will chisel your out-of-the-box thinking.

Ever traveled on Indian roads? Well, it's anything but boring! You meet the unexpected and the uncertain at every twist and turn: cows amble in coolly; street dogs bark and run in gay abandon; young sports enthusiasts play cricket in lanes; pedestrians cross roads without looking left or right; push-carts veer in alleys; speeding buses compete with one another for more passengers in carnival-ian spirit; highway drivers are blissfully unaware of traffic rules; camels and elephants often use the fast lanes; wedding chariots command the streets and hold-up traffic for hours; the car at the roundabout will stop without warning, to reset the rearview mirror or ask the neighboring car for directions; truck-drivers park vehicles on the highway just whenever they feel sleepy; and honking is a common pastime. Compared to this, American highways seem rather sane.

Yet, ask Indians living abroad and they will tell you that despite the disorder, driving on Indian roads makes them feel alert and stimulated. Actually, even Americans in India express similar sentiments! I was once traveling with a group of students from Virginia who was rather open to adventures in India. Initially, they were apprehensive during road travel, giving the crazy environment. But they soon realized that every one was aware of this madness and capable of dealing with it. So they felt protected and secure whenever driven around by an Indian chauffeur. That mental security triggered their creative liberty. So they enjoyed every other event that could have made any other foreigner anxious and stressed. This example is not meant to advocate Indian road manners! Not at all. It is just to say that you can positively respond to challenges, even in an unfamiliar terrain, with simple mind tools of inner security, mental openness and trust in other human beings. In short, by appealing to your soul, positive imagination and heart, you can be energized by all hues of life.

In fact, the bus in which these students were traveling once had a minor brush with another bus as the traffic merged. Guess what the students did? They began waving to people in the other bus and exchanged pleasantries! So you can turn a negative situation into a positive opportunity through your relaxed response. They said that their relaxed attitude was largely enabled by the calmness of the drivers of the two buses. When the buses brushed against one another, the drivers were quick to take corrective action, forgive one another and move on. When we see others as relaxed, playful and light-hearted, we are inspired to follow their better example. So our human impressionability is a creative opportunity.

Importantly, in responding to diversity, you become adept at adapting and innovating in your given set of circumstances. And that adds a lot of oomph to your imagination. You are always on the lookout to make things work, no matter what the odds. Your individual agency becomes much more proactive, enterprising and inventive. Back in the 1990s, when the Indian economy had just started to open up, a German multinational chose to start operations in India merely on the basis of the state of alertness that Indians, drivers and pedestrians alike, manifest on their roads. He said something to this effect: "If Indians can drive and navigate in this wild traffic, they have to be fully 'alive' at every moment; maintaining their nerves and focus at all times—this is where I surely want to do my business and invest!"[2]

In parts of the world, where we still find joint-families (in India, for sure), children are exposed from the start to a mini-theater of life's diversity. Living in them, one learns to cultivate sharing, value collaboration, become sensitive to the unique needs to each member, learn to resolve conflicts through adjustment and compromise, take balanced views, and become more accepting of shortcomings and forgiving of mistakes. Early exposure to the diverse realities in our world will help our children have a less rigid and in effect richer imagination. I love the college classrooms in the United States for this precisely reason: out of twenty students in a given class, at least fifteen, or more, will be representing different cultural backgrounds. In India too, a regular neighborhood is naturally diverse, both in socio-economic and cultural terms. And the diversity doesn't live in separate compartments—it's there like a vital reality that is lived through in every household. People across socio-economic groups, speaking different native languages, having different customs and faiths, are sharing a context. And like it or not, they need to get along with one another, despite the differences and idiosyncrasies.

Moreover, exposure to diversity stimulates you to exit your narrow frame of reference and become tolerant of many other ways and views. Diversity thus coaxes you to question, investigate and reflect much more than you would otherwise. It stirs you and stimulates you. Voila its role!

Therefore, diversity in your environment—different characters, surprise happenings, thwarting of plans, conflict of views, apparent upheavals et al –is offering exciting opportunities for learning and evolving, just like challenging games help children to grow up. They lead to frustrating moments as well. But this "optimal frustration" is necessary for questioning yourself and thereby evolving.

The challenging realm of diversity can then be an educating, illuminating, and transforming force in your lives. Just like hurdles in a race test and build the mettle of an athlete, likewise the stumbling blocks of diversity stretch our capacities of thinking and behavior. They can help you discover who you are and what you can be.

Your daily and different situations are natural pretexts and contexts for strengthening your creative spirit. The only requirement is that you need to see every possible context—be it a testing situation or a difficult relationship—as a learning opportunity. The moment you see something as a source of learning or energy, it turns into one.

Remember that when you get irrigated or annoyed at someone for lack of understanding, it's because you have not yet found a suitable strategy to harmonize. So your annoyance is a sign of your own inadequacy to stay balanced in conflict. Instead of getting flustered, use your trying situation as a stimulus to improve your articulation and balance.

This section gives you the tools to positively engage with diversity and allow it to positively influence you. The main tools I offer are: expanding your sense of self and well-being through awareness of your four Is; greater witnessing of your situations to learn from them; enjoining strategic thinking to see the bigger pictures and behave with your better natures; nurturing common grounds to bond better; and using friendly persuasions and playful approaches to smoothen out differences.

The tools seem simple. The real thing is the application on a day to day basis. When you can successfully apply, you will see the transformation for yourself. With practice, what seemed tough earlier will begin to look easier. But for that effortlessness to settle in eventually, you need to put in some effort to begin with! On a similar note, I remember my music teacher telling me how simple it was to sing in sync with the given rhythm and in perfect pitch and also be able improvise new melodic refrains. She wasn't wrong. With the kind of practice she had behind her, it was easy for her to juggle and coordinate all those different elements. So the way to harmony is simple. It just needs practice! With practice, an Indian proverb says, even the woolly become wise!

In conclusion, there is a need to look at diversity (of our deficiencies!) with more tolerance, love, and wisdom. Otherwise we all will want others to become like us, endorse our perspectives, and disapprove of their ways merely because they stand in stark contrast to what we believe to be good approaches. We'll become control-freaks, ridden with complacency and superiority. No matter how accomplished you are, the feelings of condescension, complacency, and that smug "I know more than you" or "I told you so," will close the gates on creative energies. But you are to let them in.

Simply accept that the realm of relationships *will remain* an unpredictable and uncertain turf. When you accept the nature of someone or something, you become more tolerant and also find inventive ways to cope. We do that with our parents and relatives all the time! So accept the fact that you will always be dealing with peculiar egos and personalities. Therefore, learn to work along with them or simply learn what you can from them. Grudge no one. Blame no one. Just walk your path with concentration on your goals and sensitivity toward your environment. You need the two in balance.

Cultivating the awareness of your larger 'I' will help you maintain this balance.

THE FOUR I'S—AWARENESS OF YOUR LARGER 'I'

You have an *impressionable* aspect, which makes you absorb and imbibe influences. Your openness makes you available to both positive and negative energies. While your spirit is susceptible to influences, your physical life is facilitated by a whole ecosystem of visible and invisible relationships. You thus have an *interconnected* reality. Then, you have an *imaginative* aspect, which is your personal software to interpret life in a way unique to you. Finally, you have an *in-play* aspect that allows you to play different roles with flexibility. While your *in-play* aspect is the most visible and creative one, it is the three previous aspects that will influence how you play and perform in the theater of life.

A quick look at all!

YOUR IMPRESSIONABLE BEING

From your genesis to your genes, from your parents to your partners, from your education to your environment, you are being created by forces beyond your conscious control. You are part of a complex field of influences that orchestrate your inner reality.

In fact, your impressionability begins in the womb itself. A third trimester fetus can feel pain and stress, to the extent that these can leave a "lasting, even lifelong imprint on the nervous system."[3] I am reminded of an episode in the Indian epic *Mahabharata* where a young warrior in the battlefield can recall an entire strategy he heard as a fetus![4] That's why pregnant mothers are asked to remain calm and happy. Parents are likewise urged not to clash in front of kids. Until the age of six, when the brain is largely operating in a hypnotic state of mind,[5] sounds and scenes are subliminally absorbed by children. Even as adults, we are highly sensitive to 'vibes' of others. They affect us before we know.

Context is contagious. You may have found yourself exclaiming like your best friend after spending a week with him or may have felt buoyed after listening to an inspiring speech. On a lighter note, I know of otherwise marriage-averse foreigners who during their stay in India become quite open to the idea of "arranged marriages," and some even commit to it after spending some time in India! On a graver note, there are instances of family-oriented people who become fanatic as a result of negative indoctrination and brainwashing.

Use your impressionability to your advantage! A foreigner friend visiting India spent a lot of time watching the have-nots. She observed that despite their miserable conditions, they had the most positive attitudes. She was so affected by their dynamism that she took some daring decisions in her own life!

Eventually, just like you guard your things, you need to guard your thoughts as well. The company of negative attitudes or people can indeed make you take to them. Mindful of that, South Koreans cook their vegetables with gentle wooden baguettes and avoid the aggressive energy of the metallic spoons.[6] Just stay aware that enduring too much negativity can risk making you negative. A music teacher who was training many out-of-tone singers found herself going off-key pretty soon! So no matter how much of an expert you are, you are still impressionable. You inner balance is a very delicate one. Watch for this instead of watching over others!

The property of energy-permeability can be used positively too. In a Gurudwara or Sikh temple, preparation of food in the free community kitchen is accompanied by constant chanting of God's name, so as to enhance positive energies. Spiked with love, a meal here tastes divine! Your positive intentions and prayers can likewise uplift another. So if you are feeling bad for someone who is ill or upset or negative, then simply send him or her your unconditional and utter love. It works like laser!

However, much as you exercise caution about the company you keep, impressions you absorb, words you use and energies you give out, beware of becoming indifferent or reclusive. To find your rhythm in a diverse world, you need to play often with it. Even in nature, the creative process is about a constant interplay between ingestion, assimilation and elimination. You too must play an active and creative role in receiving and rejecting.

Just be mindful that to evolve, you need to engage. You may have seen that home pets have trouble adjusting to the wild or street strays. That's because they never got a chance to build their strength through interaction and the natural struggle that follows between the good and the bad. Likewise, species that inbreed (or are insular) have low immunity precisely because they do not create conditions for healthy competition in their good and bad genes (and attitudes!). Therefore, allow the interaction between good and bad influences. Avoid getting rattled in moments of disagreements or differences. With positive attitudes, the friction between thoughts and energies will lead to churning of the good from the bad, and of the stronger from the weaker.

Also, give the devil its due! It is the lesser behavior that creates an opportunity to reflect upon better behavior. After all, it is only after you've had a bad experience with a fair-weather friend do you realize the true worth of your sincere friend! With your realization and thus conscious caretaking, this goodness innate in your environment will get a new lease of life.

However, even as you realize what is good in life and what isn't, maintain your openness to the fact that what is good for you may not be so good for another. I once heard a radiologist tell a patient to have a "nice and good" bladder for a clear ultrasound. But the poor patient found nothing 'good' about a bursting bladder! Likewise, what is good in one situation may not be so in another, just like woolens are good for winters but not so for summers. So be curious to find out why others find good what they do. Understanding is preferable to arguing.

Once you understand where the other is coming from, you will find that your sensibility of what is good will eventually converge with another's. That's because as humans we long for the same things—respect, love, fairness, and happiness. It's our shared soul nature.

YOUR INTERCONNECTED BEING

Just look around at the larger ecosystem and you will realize that you are benefiting from the work and caretaking of doctors, teachers, lawyers, soldiers, plumbers, and pilots, et al. But for a lot of them, you wouldn't be living so healthy or so long. However, just like an infant held in the mother's arms is ignorant of the great role she is playing in upholding it, so are most of us unaware of the great services we enjoy from the universe and our environment. In fact, we hardly ever acknowledge the contribution of our own body!

With gratitude, you can then see what you normally do not see or take for granted. The foremost way is to thank things and people at every opportunity. Dwell on the contribution of another for a couple of minutes, or just for a count of ten. Your brain and mind will register this new positive thought. So every time you eat a meal, or take a shower, thank the earth and water for their abundance and nourishing force. Or every time someone offers you even a cup of tea, thank profusely, not just for the tea but also for the care the other took in offering it to you. Or when your mother makes a meal for you, thank her labor of love with yours: give up your plans for Sunday afternoon to accommodate hers. When you feel thankful from deep within, you awaken positive feelings that help you to act kindly toward whomsoever you want.

Moreover, whenever you are in a good state of mind, use the opportunity to feel all the more thankful (for generosity comes easier in a good mood). A thumb rule I have is: thank when you are glad; sing when you are sad; forgive when you are mad!

You can also revisit a visual that reminds you of your interconnected reality. I use this mental picture of a game we played at school. It's called a three-legged race. Here, the adjacent legs of two people (standing side by side) are tied together. So if en route one falls, the other can't run either! This picture is a sharp reminder that you need to care for another's well-being in order to uphold your own.

Indeed, you need positive exchange, communication, and partnerships more for your own comfort and creativity than for the benefit of others. Even a cow alienated from its environment develops "depression and digestive disorders."[7] In the case of humans, social alienation or isolation activates "the very zones of the brain that generate ... the sting of physical pain."[8] Scientific findings confirm the healing role of relationships[9] in eliminating stress and increasing your sense of well-being. Coming home to a pet or person is reassuring. The Indian joint-family where a few generations stay together is considered a great stress-buster for those reasons. Likewise, support groups have a strong therapeutic effect on your well-being. When you can just talk and share with someone, your head feels lighter and your heart happier.

Your relationships cushion you from pain and stress. You may have noticed that is so much easier to recover from a loss or illness when you are surrounded by family and friends. Their positive words and energies help you digest your difficult experiences. Even when you do not realize the positive role of a relationship, it could still be serving you in substantial ways. For instance, you might have an aide at work with whom you do not share a bond and may not even think much of him or her. He or she may be simply answering that phone for you, bringing you a cup of tea twice a day, and taking your files from one cabin to another. But try working one day without this person, and you'll realize his or her great contribution toward sharing your workload and enabling you to concentrate on your core interests. Eventually, it doesn't matter how much another does for you. What matters is how much that helps you.

Just the mere co-presence of others, even without verbal exchange (like when you are in the midst of strangers in a mall, theater or park) is comforting. A couple visiting a sparsely populated city in the United States was rather uncomfortable throughout their stay, as they felt eerily alone while walking and driving on the empty streets. When things are empty, we don't know what to expect and that creates anxiety.

Yet we all want our space and solitude at the end of a busy and noisy day. In fact, the company of silence and emptiness is a creative opportunity to strengthen your spirit. But in solitude, we aren't exactly alone. We only replace one kind of company with another! So now you may prefer the company of books, films, or songs instead of being with people. Solitude is a just an alternate rhythm, usually a more relaxed one. This relaxation restores your vitality and then you want to go back to the stage of life again. As Martin Buber also said, "I do, indeed, close my door at times and surrender myself to a book, but only because I can open the door again and see a human face looking at me."[10]

Moreover, your solitude is pleasant because you can always have company of people at will. But ask prisoners in solitary confinement and they'll have a different story to tell. They'll tell you how much they long for contact with the world and how they feel so reassured even by the "company" of the birds that they can hear chirping outside.

Finally, just like the collective well-being of different organs is crucial for the health of the whole body, in the same our individual well-being is influenced by our collective and relational well-being. Like shown in the Hollywood movie *Avatar* (2009), we are all connected to the creative forces of the universe. To harness them, you need invoke them. Your trust, faith, positive thinking—the great forces of your imagination—will open the doors of communication between you and your creative universe.

YOUR IMAGINATIVE BEING

As an Indian guru says: "Imagination is the door through which disease as well as healing enters."[11] Cultivating a progressive imagination will make you see possibilities even in difficult situations, while a depressive imagination will make you see problems even in good times. Therefore, you need to train your imagination to picture events and process experiences in positive ways.

An example of inspired imagination is the way in which this American woman related to probably the most traumatic incident of her life. In the terror attack on two top Mumbai hotels in November 2008, what she recalled most, despite being shot, was not the trauma of it all, but the helpfulness of the hotel staff and the love and support she received from utter strangers who shared her fate. When most people had a negative picture of their experience in Mumbai, she had a most positive one; she always wanted to keep returning to India for its caring and loving people. Now, it isn't as if she wasn't traumatized by her ordeal. Who wouldn't have been? It wasn't as if she didn't go through agony, anger, suffering, and pain in those gruesome and grueling hours. But she used all these fear-causing emotions to feed a faith-generating one— the feeling of oneness she experienced with others. She chose affection over anger and hope over despair.

You too need to discourage over-critical and bitter attitudes. They are not helping you in any way. Refrain from making insensitive remarks and comments. They separate you all the more from others. Guard against your growing sense of self-importance. It will prevent your own progress. Counter your malice and meanness. They are slow poisons that eat away your vitality.

Instead, make your imagination hopeful and healthy, by habituating it to gratefulness, thoughtfulness, purposefulness and playfulness. The first will give you inner depth so that you think before judging; the second will make you sensitive so that you think before expressing; the third will make you future-oriented so that you think and act in constructive ways; while the fourth will keep you light and lively so that you keep minor stresses at bay.

For gratefulness and thoughtfulness, you need to play games with your mind to feel more connected to others than you actually are. So if you are feeling jealous someone, play a trick on your mind to see this person with more affection. You could see him or her in the image of your best friend. You will now be happy at this person's progress and not envious of it. Whenever you bring love into the picture, the force of hate abates, just as when you snuggle close for comfort, the feeling of cold subsides.

Lightheartedness and laughter will help you avoid minor irritations and stresses. So if someone tells you that you seem to have put on weight, you can have a good laugh over it, instead of feeling bad. Basically, you don't have to react and retort to everything. And certainly not when you are feeling weak and hurt!

Make your imagination purposeful and forward-oriented by having personal goals. "If you want to live a happy life, tie it to a goal, not to people or things," said Albert Einstein. When you chase goals, you think in more constructive ways than destructive. Dreams and goal fire your imagination and help you think bigger and better.

In general, keep your imagination uplifted by opening it to inspiration. Read stories of courage and achievement. Or be in the company of people who exude optimism and enterprise. What I also find quite valuable is listening to myself in moments when I am offering advice to others (and they may not be listening!). When it comes to telling others what to do, we really have some brilliant ideas!

Finally, you need a wholesome imagination to play well to all sorts of challenges in a diverse and dynamic environment.

YOUR IN-PLAY BEING

To paraphrase jazz singer, Louis Armstrong, life is what you play.

Each one of you has a rich and diverse inner world. You have an innate capacity to express in many ways. As per Indian metaphysics, your have been through 8.4 million incarnations, rather different stages of evolution, before becoming a human being. It follows, as Swami

Satyananda Saraswati says, that "we have all assumed different postures in our various incarnations."[12]All kinds of feelings find a place in you. But it is up to you to give the pride of place to some.

To have a more conscious approach to what roles you favor or prefer, you need become aware of the limits and possibilities of different ones. For instance, if you adopt the stance of a rival vis-à-vis your colleagues, you will tend to think in critical ways and express yourself in combative ways. Instead, if you favor the stance of a friend or ally, even in competitive contexts, then you will help yourself to think and relate with more generosity.

Now the roles that you play or choose will not remain limited to you. They will affect the choice of others too. Others usually choose stances that are an extension of yours. So if you are being a friend, others too will adopt friendly roles.

But sometimes, despite your best intentions, others feel upset with you because of their own insecurity, fear or envy. What should you do in such cases? You should be yourself even more. Rather, you should strengthen the roles that you believe in. Instead of becoming disappointed or dejected, you should become even strongly committed to your positive vision. The negative role played by the other –of not responding nicely to you—would then have played a positive role.

Indian thought urges you to see every situation and every character, be they 'good' or 'bad', as part of the grand *lila* or drama of life. Different people and situations will keep coming your way and going away. They are all part of the story. And they have to adhere by their entries and exits. So don't feel upset when someone's part is over. In a situation of a breakup or betrayal, thank the other for whatever roles he or she played, and eagerly look forward to the next scene and new characters!

On the same note, you will meet all kinds of characters and be challenged by all sorts of situations. What should you do in order to face them well? Use your smartness and sensitivity to respond in ways that leave us all better off. Aren't you thrilled when in a drama the hero gives a fitting response to the villain? Aren't you relieved when the villain has a moment of realization? Of course! So you need to think and respond in ways that bring about healing and understanding. But you can't do so if you get hurt, blame others, lose your cool, complain or cry foul. To play well, you have to first become a good sport!

The first step is to see the roles played by others, even the villainous ones, in a tolerant spirit. See others as your co-actors on the stage of life. Instead of grudging them their roles, use your time and energy to improve your act. Now ordinarily, we get so incensed by the negative actions of others that we forget our own lines and lose our own direction! It is due to this frailty on our part that the negative succeeds in making us negative. But shouldn't it be the other way round?

It will be so when you use the trigger of a negative situation to turn even more toward your positive core. So whenever you spot something that you dislike, use your reaction foremost to reject similar behavior in yourself. For example, a young schoolboy who played the role of a cruel king wondered later whether he too behaved cruelly with this cat, for he would shoot pellets at it every time it went to sleep under his father's car. He immediately stopped doing it because he realized that it was a 'cruel' thing to do. In fact, he now caresses the cat whenever it comes.

So the negative behavior of the king made this boy improve his own conduct in another sphere. Ergo, negative situations will only get the better of you if you become negative yourself while handling them. But if you learn from them instead, then you will eventually get the better of them.

So you need to arrive at a mindset of enjoying the pressures and challenges posed by diverse people and situations. You will then begin to value the chorus of your co-actors on the stage of life and see them all as fuelling your growth.

To visualize how you need to go about handling situations that risk agitating you, see this case. I remember this incident with a bank teller where he was so reluctant to help me and in fact kept posing obstacle after obstacle in my way. My ego wanted to give it back to him. But I was aware that the ego is an energy-guzzler. It will use up all my good energy (or good karma as we say in India) and leaves me feeling spent and exhausted. That's like spending your hard-earned savings for nothing! Mythological stories tell us of the perils of cursing others. When yogis spent their accumulated spiritual powers for cursing others, their words would come true but at the cost of depleting their own strength. Not a good bargain!

So to prevent such follies from your end, use the tool of patience and acceptance. See the way I did in this case. I accepted the teller the way he was instead of getting annoyed with him. To help myself accept, I recalled my larger purpose for being here (to get my work done!) and also saw the teller as my kin. As a result, my waning concentration returned and my stance softened. I found myself appreciating his objections and smiling at him, notwithstanding his rudeness and frowns. Basically, before he could pick a fight, I handed the olive branch. Eventually, he relented. In fact, he smiled. So did I!

Acceptance is not about inaction. It is about taking corrective action through mature means. It enables your flexibility and inventiveness. Just like a flexi-chair allows you more mobility and scope, your flexibility will similarly stimulate you to bend forward or backward in response to the need of the hour without affecting your balance. As you become flexible, new dimensions will become accessible.

To play roles with acceptance and to overcome your anger, you can use smart moves along with mind games. Consciously step into contexts that necessitate your calm. For instance, go out accompanied by your child. The setting of you as the parent, protector and role model will put your aggression in the back seat. You'll have to find other means to cope!

Also become aware of the contexts that you are entering. So for instance, if you are largely among competitors, maintain more of your collaborative stances. Competitive energies usually make the environment less benevolent. Counter the imbalance by having stances that will put you and others at ease.

Finally, each role is like a different asana or posture that stimulates you in different ways. Knowing how different roles affect you, you need to adopt them with awareness. In yoga, you are aware that bending forward helps you to surrender and relax while bending backwards stimulates your confidence and generosity. So you call upon them depending on your needs. Gradually, you will know what kind of roles to veer toward in different situations. Actually, in our hearts of hearts, we all know which way to go. We just need a motivated and generous spirit to rise above our ego and play the greater parts we are capable of. The next chapter offers help!

GAMES FOR HARMONIZATION

An ancient Chinese perspective says that it is in living out a relationship, such as between mother and child, husband and wife, teacher and student, between siblings, and among friends that you enhance your ability to adjust, accommodate, and become tolerant and wise. However, since adjusting and accommodating do not come easily to us, we tend to lose patience or act with narrow vision. The stimulus for relating positively can be found through creative orientations and games. Dr. Eric Berne's *Games People Play* revealed to us the kind of manipulative power equations that we are all playing with one another. Yet, games that you play for positive purposes and with a heart can be a win-win. The next chapter has some neat ideas for all!

Talent develops in tranquility, character in the full current of human life.
—Johann Wolfgang Von Goethe

CHAPTER 5

GAMES YOU CAN PLAY!

Changing your responses from negative to positive isn't such a challenge. You just need better ways to manage your mind and emotions. As you follow some rules in the game of your life, you will learn manage your inner commotion with the ease of a traffic guard.

To diagnose your current level of awareness, answer the following, honestly. My comments are in brackets!

Q: Do you find it difficult to forget someone's hurtful words?

A: Yes. (And even wait for opportunities for tit-for-tat!)

Q: Do you need much persuasion to say sorry to someone?

A: Yes. (We'd rather get the other's apology first!)

Q: Are you miserly with your compliments and generous with your criticism?

A. Not really. (Read that as a resounding yes!)

Q: Do you become jealous and envious of others?

A: Hmmm. (C'mon! we all are awed by another's success. However, we can turn the awe into inspiration, and go beyond the envy.)

Q: Do you have an exaggerated sense of what you've done for others but have a shrunken sense of what you've received from them or from your life?

A: Don't know... (Absolutely! We even attempt to undo the favors done by another by 'justifying' that he or she owed it to us in any case!)

Now answer this last one: do you want at least one relationship in your life to become a source of strength and stability? If yes, then we'll need to rework the above responses. Actually, we'll have to radically change them!

I offer a bouquet and blend of creative approaches under the umbrella of "Loving Strategies." All have a common aim—to enrich your rapport with your loved ones, and also your casual acquaintances. Who knows, they too might become your loved ones one day!

LOVING STRATEGIES—A CONSCIOUS APPROACH TO CURB NEGATIVE BEHAVIOR AND FOSTER CREATIVE EXCHANGE

Ordinarily, we keep our relationships, even the good ones, on a junk diet of taunts, nagging, nitpicking, irritable tones and impatience. You need to instead boost their health and vitality with understanding, appreciation, respectful stances, sincerity, warmth and playfulness. When you can do so with people you like, then you'll beautify your bond. When you can do so with people you do not like, you will beautify yourself.

To do so, I suggest and discuss the following:

- **Witnessing Situations:** Learning Opportunities for Your Head and Heart

- **Strategic Thinking:** For Sensibility and Sensitivity

- **Strategic Tactics:** To Harness the Best Possible in People

- **Common Grounds:** Nurturing Bonds

- **Playfulness:** Lighthearted Feedback

WITNESSING SITUATIONS: LEARNING OPPORTUNITIES FOR YOUR HEAD AND HEART

What looks annoying from close quarters is engaging from a distance. So if you are fighting with your partner, you will be annoyed, but those who are watching you will be entertained!

This habit of watching what's happening is not insensitive. It helps you to become more sensitive to the dynamics at play. From a distance then, you can see the situation better, sift through the issues better and sort out matters better.

Cultivate the habit of distancing or witnessing in your daily situations. You will discover ways to heal yourself and your relationships.

Firstly, witnessing will make you see your own exaggerated reactions. This realization can be a turning point.

To cultivate the habit of witnessing, turn into an observer when moving among your friends, colleagues or strangers. It's easier to watch others to begin with! For instance, use the opportunity of waiting at a hospital or restaurants to look at how different people behave. So if the waiter got a wrong dish by mistake, some will laugh about it and some will get upset. Reflect upon what you see. Think of what you might have done in a similar situation. Watch yourself thinking through matters. Behold your own values. Become more aware of what kind of responses you prefer. Now wonder if there is a mismatch between what you prefer in a cooler state of mind and what you might proffer in the heat of the moment. Make efforts to bridge the gap. Also, such mental exercises will prepare you to deal with similar situations in other spheres with more consideration and less impulse.

In a related application, make detached commentary in ordinary situations in order to educate your spirit via your own insight. For instance, I once spilled some water on the floor and went running for a mop to clear the mess. A kind lady standing there reassured me that she couldn't even see the spilt water and so asked me to let things be. Habituated to witnessing my situations, I playfully told her "since I had caused the mess, I could see its fallout, and knew where I was at fault, even if that was not apparent to others." She smiled with a knowing look, as if reflecting on some event in her own life. Look at this way. You are going to make some comments in any case. If you express with a little more depth, you can turn it in a healing opportunity for someone in some way. Moreover, every situation has a lesson sealed into it. Take a good look and you'll find what it is.

Secondly, the habit of watching yourself in action and expression can help you overcome your conditioned reflexes For example, if you find yourself exclaiming, "Can't you see!" every time someone bumps into you, then question your reaction. Resist from justifying yourself. For that'll keep you glued to old ways of thinking and doing. But we want to find better ways! So refuse to justify. Seek only to understand. To understand better, situate your response in different scenarios. Ask yourself: how would you have responded if this man was your father or relative? Wouldn't you have been more sensitive and tolerant? Or what if he was your boss? Wouldn't you have been more cheerful about it, and likely to have said "I am sorry" even if it wasn't your fault? Such sobering reflection can help you reset your reflexes.

You can help others as well to question their conditioned responses by interrogating their assumptions. Take an instance of this young girl who was depressed at being left by her boyfriend for someone else. Her hurt and shock were understandable. But then she had to move on, right? Yet she wasn't ready to come out of her self-pity zone. So I used some mind games for challenging her feelings. I asked her what if she was the one who had fallen in love with someone else while she was with her ex? Wouldn't she have prayed and prayed that he would find someone else? Yes, she nodded. And smiled! That realization freed her of her grudges and made her accept her situation without malice.

Take another example where a young woman found answers to a nagging problem by witnessing her good responses in one situation and then transferring them to another problematic one. Now she was facing a lot of trouble with her mother-in-law (universal story!). The problem was that the mother-in-law wanted attention and so did the daughter-in-law! A year passed with cold vibes standing in between them. They just suffered each other during festive and family gatherings. The relationship was blocked.

One day, the daughter-in-law invited her parents for dinner. She witnessed her own behavior vis-à-vis her own parents. She realized that she was rather patient and generous when it came to handling the idiosyncrasies of her own parents. If her mother wanted the soup warmer, the daughter rushed to do so; if her father said he wanted more salt, she added some without ado. Later she wondered how she might have felt and reacted if her mother-in-law had made the same requests or observations. She would have felt offended. But why did she not make a big deal of it with her own parents? She realized that she was a part of the problem.

She resolved to respond to her mother-in-law as if she were her own mother. This strategic intervention enabled her to become more tolerant and indulgent toward her mother-in-law. Her generous behavior was not lost on her mother-in-law. The latter heartily reciprocated. She began to bake the cakes that her daughter-in-law loved and would offer to look after the grandchildren whenever the daughter-in-law needed to travel. Their relationship didn't just unblock. It took off!

The final aspect of witnessing is your budding vigilance. Interpersonal and environmental awareness is your biggest protection. An Indian proverb says that is much more beneficial to secure yourself (like you secure your house) instead of blaming others for hurting you.

So take stock of the stage and characters before jumping to play in it. However, patiently collect your facts before jumping to conclusions. For instance, see others behave in different situations before you make up your mind about them. Also, sometimes you might not like someone initially but might form a positive opinion upon discovering his or her good deeds at a later point in time. Eventually, expand your understanding with your insight instead of rushing to form opinions and announce judgments. And as Prof. Sue Evans says, "As long as we do not understand, why should we judge? And once we do understand, why should we judge?"[13]

The whole purpose of witnessing is that you should be able to play and act in your field from a more informed standpoint. So that you can influence how situations shape up and how people behave.

STRATEGIC THINKING: FOR SENSIBILITY AND SENSITIVITY

Strategic thinking is not just for managing your business. It can equally be used to manage your relationships.

By cultivating it, you will begin to think and act carefully, thoughtfully and purposefully to passing or recurring problems in situations and relationships. Then at least, you will not brew more trouble from existing trouble. And at best, you will turn around the troubles into opportunities for better engagement.

The first step is acceptance and tolerance. With acceptance, you won't jump to judging and will take the calmer and objective route of witnessing. That way you will look upon situations as if they are cases to be solved!

Your acceptance will make you more charitable. Let's take the case of your employee X who has done something that has annoyed you. In your initial anger, you might have wanted to shout at X. But your acceptance of X will change your reaction. You will now want to do something like, "making X understand his mistake." In this slightly more tolerant mode, you are also likely to remind yourself of some positive qualities of this person. Maybe he is loyal, but is careless sometimes. You will now refer yourself to this overall situation before taking steps to address the issue.

Had you acted upon your initial irritation, you would have messed up your situation even more and perhaps lost out on a good employee. Anger, annoyance, and impatience narrow our vision. Acceptance expands it a little bit.

Empathy, the second aspect of strategic thinking, will uplift your vision radically, as then your heart will come more into the picture. Now in case of your own child, if he or she did something that annoyed you, won't you figure out a way to handle with care, reasonableness and understanding? Unless you are short on patience or troubled by some stresses of your own, you are likely give good advice and take firm steps to improve his or her performance. With empathy, we tend to think of 'You' as much as 'I,' which balances the rapport. With empathy, negative coercion is replaced by positive persuasion.

Moreover, without empathy, we are tempted to pigeon-hole others as selfish or bad and thus not look it them with due consideration. But with empathy, you see with a sense of proportion. Now if you have a girlfriend who is dominating or rude, you wouldn't rubbish her as 'bad'. Your greater indulgence and affection will make you something like: "I know she can be rude, but she is really good at heart."

To engage your empathy for strangers or casual acquaintances, play mind games with yourself. So if you are feeling disgusted at the man who puked in the bus, picture him immediately as your father or brother. You feel see how quickly the right course of action will come to your mind. Instead of making a face, you will be making a move to help.

Evidently, strategic thinking is hardly at odds with sensitive thinking. In fact, acceptance and empathy enable strategic thinking to lead to exalted thinking.

But you may also ask: why do I have to play games with my mind? What's wrong with speaking my mind? You need to realize that everything that crosses your mind is not necessarily your mind, nor is everything healthy for your mind. Do you eat everything you can? You choose and discern, right? Do the same for what you feed your mind. Even a nightmare is a thought that crosses your mind, but would you like to hold on to it? Wouldn't you be relieved if you could erase it from your mind? Wouldn't you make that extra effort to do that visualization exercise your therapist advises? Mind games with your own mind are also meant to free you of negative feelings that arise from a narrow sense of self. By connecting to the other with empathy, you see them as an extended part of your reality and thus handle them with sensitivity. In the bargain, your thoughts, feelings and values are all uplifted.

Now there is nothing wrong with feeling whatever you may be feeling in a certain situation. But if it is threatening your balance instead of inspiring you, then please question and nudge it. And then you will find that you can have so many different responses to the same situation. You are free to choose.

This Indian parable is instructive in telling us how you can even have entirely different responses to the same situation, just based on the different light thrown on them from moment to moment. Look at this man. He is reacting to his house burning in front of his eyes. Upon seeing his house burning, he is traumatized and frozen; upon being told by his son that he had actually sold the house a day before, he is overjoyed; in the very next moment, upon being told by his younger son that the sale-deal is only on paper and not yet materialized, the man is once again inconsolable; and finally, upon the prospective buyer arriving on scene, the mourning man is over the moon. So your feelings are flowing in any case. With mind games, you will play an active and conscious part in this flow.

It is of course challenging to play mind games vis-à-vis people against whom you have bias or prejudice. How do you remain malice-free and forgiving toward, let's say your neighbor who is prying into your privacy for juicy gossip? Or how can you stay patient toward your subordinate who repeatedly gives you flimsy excuses for coming late to work? Or how can you be generous with your superior who plays petty games to hog all credit for your work?

If playing games with your mind seems difficult to begin with, try distracting it. Just like you do not answer your cell phone every time it rings, you do not have to react to every thought that crosses your mind or everything that another does. Take your attention somewhere else. Call up your pal, go for a movie or a walk, spray perfume and look dapper, take a shower, or share a pizza with a friend.

But just know that the harder it gets, the better it is! When dealing with people who are inimical or jealous or dominating or with whom you have baggage, you will need to maintain the loving part of strategy all the more. In doing so, you will call upon greater empathy and expand its role in your life.

Eventually, for empathy to come naturally to us, we need to make efforts early in our lives. An Indian actor once gave a moving account of how his mother taught him to be concerned even about his opponents in game. So when he would return home after winning a match, she would congratulate him for his victory, but would also ask him how the boy who lost to him. She would remind him that this boy too had a family and his sadness will make his mother sad as well. She urged him to befriend is opponent and share his sorrow and cheer him up. As a result, he began to see others with a soul.

Especially in our competitive culture, we need to remain acutely aware of not trampling over others in our quest for growth. An ex-navy Indian officer shared this beautiful motto with me. He recalls it from his days at the National Defense Academy, where it was inscribed in the cricket pavilion. And it says: "And when the great scorer writes the score against your name, it is not whether you won or lost, but how you played the game." Life is not just about what you do, but also about how you do.

There will always be people you find negative or hot to handle. It is your prerogative to engage with them or not. Do so without calling others 'bad.' Also it is easy to avoid, escape and label others as bad. But ask yourself, how many people will you keep avoiding? There is always some fault to be found with others. Even your dear friends or members of family have traits that bother you. And you can't even quit them!

You need to be aware that engagement is necessary for growth while escaping gives you much needed rest. So consciously decide upon your 'escape-engage' mix, just like you decide how many hours you will work and for how many will you rest.

So the final aspect of strategic thinking involves making considered choices about people and relationships. I use a 60-40 mark to decide whether or not to pursue a relationship. So if I find enough good aspects, then I endure the bitter half too! To challenge myself, I sometimes consider cases of 40-60 too! But do place limits on your endurance. If you try to work with weights that you can't handle, you might hurt yourself.

And yes, continue to be kind toward all. Remain mindful that if you are avoiding some people, it's only because you can't handle them or haven't found suitable ways, and not because they are rejects.

In fact, if you can find a way to keep your heart peaceful even when you are among stressful people and situations, you will develop such endurance that you will tough to break down in routine challenges. In fact, it is good to see your difficult relationships in your past in the same spirit. If you find yourself patient today, it's probably because someone made the going tough for you!

STRATEGIC TACTICS: TO HARNESS THE BEST POSSIBLE IN PEOPLE

Focus on what is good in others. When you affirm a good quality in someone, you confirm it for yourself and the other. Also, when you tell others about what is good in them, they are motivated to tell you what is good in you. An energizing give and take ensues.

There is a pretty story to inspire us to see with kindness. There was once a fine pot and a fractured one.[14] One day, the lesser pot, feeling inferior to the greater pot, said to its master: "I have not served you well. You fill me with water till the top, but I am unable to deliver it all as most of it leaks out en route." The water bearer lovingly pats the pot and tells it, "I am grateful to your leaking nature. Due to it, one barren side of the road has got irrigated and is now teeming with flowers!" The cracked pot wasn't just comforted by this response but also found a new sense of self-worth and purpose.

Like the water bearer, you too can focus on the good aspects of people and thereby help them focus on the same. However, give appreciation to energize, not to further conceit. Prefer to praise the qualities of the heart. Praise for the head usually goes to the head!

To improve someone's behavior, guide him or her toward goals that will require him or her to make independent decisions on some path of learning and growth. A personal experience can lead one to deep understanding and realization. So summon your visual thinking to see how you can create new structures and dynamics in place. Just sermons won't suffice!

Then, to improve your good relationships, give them a goal-orientation. Ask yourself, what is the prime purpose of your togetherness? With your greater priority in the picture, you will negotiate and compromise in healthier ways. Now, if you were helping another couple to resolve some marital issues, how would you handle their histrionics over minor points (which may be looking like major points to them!)? Quite the same way that you'd handle chewing gum in your kid's hair—remaining focused on getting it out of there, and not getting distracted or bogged down by his or her intermittent oohs and aahs. Do ditto in your friendships.

Better still, give a strategic vision to your partnership. Find a shared aim to achieve, like: helping one another to become more compassionate human beings. A broader vision makes narrow ones ineffective. So chances are that with a greater vision in your midst, you will not fight over where to place the new chairs in the living room. I am not saying you won't ever have fights. But now you are likely to negotiate playfully, instead of arguing stubbornly. In creative living, fights are fun!

For your casual interactions too—going out to a party, sharing lunch with a colleague, watching a film with a friend, calling up a friend, receiving a guest at home—think about the direction of your interaction. Reflect for a couple of minutes over your main purposes in the given time and opportunity. For instance, before stepping into your office, you could meditate for a moment on this: "I have nine hours to achieve my best. Let me only think and act in ways that help me." A more defined direction will help you have greater concentration on your work as well as greater tolerance vis-à-vis office politics.

In a related application, create role definitions to avoid expecting everything from everyone. Define the roles of your various friends and acquaintances in your life: "Lisa is someone I can laugh with"; "Sonia is a wonderful neighbor who is happy to baby-sit for me when I need"; "I like walking with Maya because her good speed paces me up as well." Such role-definitions will place a cap on your expectations. Without them, you might expect Sonia to walk as fast as Maya, or expect Maya to make you laugh the way Lisa can. That's a bit like ruing that a mango doesn't taste like a papaya!

Moreover, recognize Sonia's contribution to your well-being through the role she plays in safe-keeping the keys of your house. Appreciate her positive role, instead of just treating her as a good for nothing, or "just someone you leave your keys with." Your appreciation of her limited role can actually motivate her to expand her role in your life.

As a corollary, simply focus on the major roles that people play in your life. This will not make your interactions half-hearted but much more wholesome. So let's say, you are facing problems in relating positively to your father. The bone of contention is that you are dissatisfied with his approaches to running his business, while he too does not trust your acumen. This situation is creating stresses and preventing genuine exchange. To breakthrough, why not just focus on your father's greatest role? He is, after all, the breadwinner for the entire family, and without that you wouldn't be where you are. When you can focus on this major role and brush aside unrelated thoughts, you'll actually become more of a friend to him. And he will be moved to respond sympathetically as well. With a positive strategic role, you can open up a whole new chapter in your relationship.

Also, respect the (unflattering!) truth that you can't be your partner's one-stop relationship, and nor should you expect the other to be that for you. Compose the stage of your life by peopling it with a variety of relationships and a host of engaging pursuits. You will lighten the load of expectation on that one relationship. And its fuse won't go off!

Role-definitions can especially make you more tolerant about what you do not like in the other. For example, you may find this person you walk with as boastful and greedy. But since you have limited your interaction to the common ground of walking, and aren't expecting anything more than a pleasant walking experience, you will be able to deal with his or her boastful behavior with more tolerance.

Goal and role-limitations will eventually help you become more accepting of the overall mix of strengths and weaknesses in people. You will not expect a hundred percent from every one. You will learn to accept both the greater and lesser in others as a package deal.

Play roles, even uncharacteristic ones, but with a positive intention to improve another's state of mind or any given situation. An example concerns a lonely lady who was prone to negative thinking. She would always greet me with her list of woes; most of them imagined (quite like us all!). No amount of counseling or motivation from my end seemed to work. One day, I tried a strategic role-reversal. I dropped my usual perennial role of a motivator and adopted one that resembled her. This time around, it was I who propped up a problem and asked her for a solution. Smart move! In responding to my woes, she unwittingly turned into a healer. Her whole demeanor and expression became enthused as she began to give me recipes that would spur my appetite. I saw her confident energies overtake her meek ones. And I gained as well. I was thoroughly nourished with all the care and attention that flowed toward me, given that fact that I had assumed a receptive role.

Now strategic and smart moves are not at odds with sincere behavior and straight talk. But every one does not share the same level of awareness. As an Indian proverb says, if you think that a monkey will understand sermons, then you are the one who is behaving foolishly! So you have to use the means that will enable the other. And that is why you need to think of suitable strategic interventions and smart moves. They will help pave the way for harmonious and honest exchange.

To inspire your strategic moves, and not fall for petty manipulations and egoistic temptations to control others, play your situation-specific roles in conjunction with greater positive roles. To know what greater roles you prefer, ask yourself what you would like to be or do, if you were free to choose. You will find yourself aiming for parental and benevolent roles. Think of a person or a role model who has what you like and bear this image in mind at all times. Let's say you like someone who is generous with his advice and mentors you even as he corrects you. So in case of a situation where you need to sort out matters with a subordinate, engage this greater role of a friend and guide. As a result, you will not just address the given situation but also go beyond it. You will not overreact to the problem and will see the situation from the other person's shoes as well. The other too, moved by your sincerity and sensitivity, will now receive your critical feedback in a positive spirit.

Make such positive roles your perennial 'default' or your 'home page'! So always start from here and return to them. That way you won't get lost when playing your situation-specific roles. In fact, whenever you feel stumped by a situation or feel lost, take refuge in your perennial positive role. When you take the higher pedestal, it is difficult to stoop low!

You can also stimulate others to step into their greater and generous roles. An important way is to make them feel warmer in the relationship. To establish the warmth, maintain caring tones and stances. Another good way is to often use the mantra of a relational name. For instance, when you address your brother called Josh as simply "brother," then you will stimulate him to play a brotherly role toward you. You can even address a dear friend as brother and it will have a similar effect. You can also use special nicknames for your close friends. While hearing your ordinary name alerts, hearing your special name elates! And when people are in a good mood, feel that they are in a loving and trusting environment; they are ready to give their utmost.

And now just one last problem to be dealt with: what if others take your good nature for granted? What if you are always treated like a doormat and taken for a ride? Well, others can only take you for a ride if you let them! Moreover, if you are falling into the same traps over and over again, then you need to improve your own eyesight instead of blaming others!

Also, you need to tell others when they are crossing their lines. Or perhaps they are crossing the lines because you haven't put them in place!

Then, maybe you make yourself look weak and vulnerable to others and thus tempt them to run over you. An ancient Indian story is illustrative. Once there was a snake that would threaten to hurt the children playing in the fields. The kids, rather sad, stopped playing in the fields. One day, a sage passes by and notices the pulled-down faces of the children. The children narrate their woes regarding the snake. The wise man goes to the snake and gently explains to him that he should not bite the children and let them play in peace. The snake respects the sage and gives his word to not hurt the children. The children are elated. The next day, they start playing and realize that the snake is not bothering them at all. Taking that to be his weakness, they start pelting stones at him in glee. The snake gets badly hurt, but conscious of his promise, he refrains from retaliating. The same continues to happen for a couple of days. By now the snake is badly wounded and is lying helpless in a corner. Just then the old sage comes by again. He is shocked to see the snake in that state. He administers first aid to him, and then asks him how all this came to pass. The snake weakly narrates to him how based on the promise given to the sage he did not retaliate when the boys began to hit him. The sage smiles and says, "I stopped you from biting and hurting others. Not from hissing and scaring them away!"

Anyway, before you 'hiss,' please examine your own context! Are you are in a commanding position? Are you in a supportive environment? Are people willing to listen to you? Even if you put your right foot forward but at the wrong time and place, you may be courting trouble.

Another Caveat: strategies meant to scare risk heating up your head and can make you lose your balance and calm. On a scientific note, "When you pretend to feel a certain way, your brain produces the chemicals to match and, before you know it, you actually DO feel that way."[15] That means good news when you play positive roles, but spells trouble when you assume the negative ones. Actor Anthony Hopkins, aware of the dangers of acting out negative states of mind, opines that the negative roles he plays for screen lead him to depressive moods in real life.[16] For your body and brain, roles played or emotions imagined are rather real. So, when you laugh, smile, or cheer up another, you actually start feeling good. But the flip side is that when you show your anger or disapproval, you actually become annoyed and irritable.

Therefore, use-disciplining stances like a pinch of pepper in your larger positive role repertoire. And always keep cooling roles handy to counterbalance your surging passion. Also sweeten the bitter pill that you might be giving to another, just the way moms mash a medicinal tablet into a sweet banana so that the baby eats it without feeling the bad taste. Positive packaging and conscious balancing will take the sting out of your disciplining roles. So for instance, if you are giving your critical point of view to someone, counterbalance it by agreeing to some of his or her suggestions as well. When you put one bad apple in a dozen, it will be hardly noticed, or patiently suffered!

All in all, whether you are in a powerful position or not, direct hissing should be a resort of exception, and not become the norm. If you use it indiscriminately, you will end up offending others more than defending yourself. As others feel humiliated or offended, they will become all the more negative toward you. That's akin to multiplying your enemies. Not smart!

It is far more prudent and sustainable to develop tactics for indirect hissing. You needn't nuke it like antibiotics when milder antiseptics can help. So proactively place strategic deterrents in place. Make your boundaries clear. Exemplify the standards of behavior that you expect from others. You can also carry your security and support systems with you to not become overly anxious or fearful. For instance, if you are wary of your aggressive colleague, meet her with another colleague whom she is scared of!

Now despite your best intentions and best understanding, you will still mess up some roles and rhythms. But rest assured that just as a tailor's hands become skilled and speedy with experience and cut a fabric more or less right, so will you become a super loving strategist soon enough.

Remember the bottom-line that if you want support, you have to win hearts and not alienate them. And you will succeed only when make others feel good about themselves. As a poem by Erich Fried says, "I love you for the sake of my better self that you know how to bring out."[17]

For the next level of harmonizing, bond over common interests.

COMMON GROUNDS: NURTURING BONDS

Will a plant give you flowers just because you've bought it? Not at all. Effectively, it needs your care to blossom. So do your relationships.

A common ground is a way to inch closer to your heart and another's - by participating in common interests. So if two friends are meeting over a cup of coffee, they can enhance their interaction by doing something they both enjoy, like making music or reading poetry or playing scrabble. Their communication will then revolve around a common peg, channeling their interaction. They will also feel more fraternal toward one another. As a result, forbearance and patience will go up whereas envy and jealousy will reduce. On such a favorable and fertile ground, you can grow many new things.

What if two or more people do not have much in common? Take the instance of a father-son relationship where the father is interested in teaching his son tennis while the boy is much more interested in music. The common ground seems to be nil in this case as both are interested in different things. But a closer look will make you discover a much more vital bond—their care for each other. And when we care, our interests become elastic. We can participate in activities that the other loves.

In our example, despite the father's fancy for sports, his love for his son will make him at least an interested listener while his son is playing the piano. This leaning forward may even spur him to ask to son for music a lesson (which would create a delightful role reversal—the child can chide the father and the father can dutifully follow the son's instructions!). Having extended his understanding to his son, the father is now in a better position to ask the same of his son. And the son will too feel obliged to reciprocate!

So the son may now agree to join his dad in a game of tennis after all. The father then can strategically strike up similarities between a game of tennis and playing the piano, such as the coordination of the mind and body required by both. Now it's quite possible that the child will continue to prefer piano to tennis. The aim is hardly to convert others to our interests. It is simply to participate with curiosity and openness in what another likes. If you like it as well, even better!

What about cases where there is neither shared love nor a common interest? That can happen sometimes in your workplace. Perhaps you have a colleague who you want to get to know better but he seems cold and aloof. But if you want to know him, woo him! Just step up your inclination to learn about your colleague's interests. Perhaps he likes good food and you like to cook! So design an event with the intention of bonding. Even verbally referring to shared and familiar grounds can help you catch another's attention. So you can even start a discussion about different kinds of curries and spices to get your distant colleague to participate more animatedly.

Take cue from the interests of others to expand your interest-repertoire. Why be so rigid about what you like and dislike? For instance, even if you are not very interested in animals, you can always accompany someone who is. You may not still fall in love with animals but might chance upon an idea to sell fashion accessories for pets. Inspiration can come anytime and anywhere!

Even if you cannot explore other interests—we all have limits on time and resources—you can be open, curious and respectful toward what others do. Isn't it great that our world has so many people who are interested in different things? Life is colorful because of this variety. Play with it! Moreover, the more you encourage others to be the best of what they can be or want to be, the more will they seek your company and counsel.

But what should you do if some habits of the other irritate or annoy you? Tolerate what you can and tease lovingly about what you can't. Steadily replace bad vibes, annoyed tones, sarcastic remarks and angry looks with hearty laughter and playful banter.

PLAYFULNESS: LIGHTHEARTED FEEDBACK

Differences are here to stay. In opinion, thought, and feeling, no two people will think or act alike. Whereas as kids, we enjoyed our playtime and resolved differences with alacrity and agility, as adults we began to cling to our grudges and express in sarcastic and hurtful ways. We are now more concerned with preserving our egos and less about perpetuating the play.

Yet it is the spirit of play that can help us connect positively with the grand diversity around us. Dr. Stuart Brown, a long-time researcher on the role of play our lives, gives this endearing example of how this polar bear and a female husky, who usually have a predatory relationship, actually end up having a playful one, based on the husky's signals to play. The joy of play subsumes our survival instincts and helps us override our mistrust toward one another. If the promise of playful interaction can lead these two unlikely teammates to go beyond the "huge asymmetry of power," as Dr. Brown says, it can certainly help us humans to bond with people who are different than us. As Dr. Brown says, play allows us to "explore the possible."[18]

You may have felt a spontaneous emergence of playfulness at a get-together of friends, with all that playful banter of teasing one another and random leg-pulling. Playfulness is a lighthearted way of brushing against each other's boundaries, using healthy humor and loving laments. When you prefix your complaints with tones of care and concern, you buy another's receptivity. If you criticize without caring, you will make the other defensive. So do not express to just pass of your stress to the other. Think strategic. Become conscious of why you want to say what you wish to and how you can improve your delivery of your message. Conscious exercise of playfulness and engaging humor will dampen your stress and cushion it for the other. A bit like a pillow fight!

Playful attitudes will help you smoothly iron out grouses, without making a big deal of it. For example, if your son is ruing you that you left him alone to study while you went out for dinner, you can playfully remind him of the particular night when he was trying hard that you all leave him alone at home, so that he could invite some friends over!

Moreover, such exchanges will reduce your reliance on gossiping, since you would be taking the positive steps of openly and lightly bringing up your issues with the person concerned. In fact, by disallowing lurking suspicions and negativity to fester and foam up in your mind, you will strengthen your relationships as well. As the poet Blake says in his poem *The Poison Tree*, "I was angry with my friend: I told my wrath, my wrath did end. I was angry with my foe: I told it not, my wrath did grow."

By allowing playfulness, you will gradually wipe out spiteful and sore behavior on your own part. Instead, you will express your doubts and ask questions, minus the negative vibes and jibes.

Playfulness among life partners is rather productive. In married couples, where expectations from each other run high (unsustainably so), a conscious pursuit of playfulness, even on touchy topics, can help partners eliminate the dark zones of nagging and below-the-belly remarks. That would help them relate to each other foremost as good friends, which will surely energize their usual roles of husband or wife. On grounds of friendliness, conversations will not lead to clashes but actually become therapeutic. Ordinarily, since communication gets cramped in marriages, partners end up playing cat-and-mouse-games, which take them away from each other. Playful interaction can once again bring them closer. It will even revive the romance!

Significantly, in a context of playfulness, we tend to express our emotions the way we use emoticons in emails or text messages—feeling that way a bit, but also ready to feel better. So we are quick to switch our sulking to smiling in a matter of seconds. Playfulness thus enables a healthy balance of attachment and detachment.

Some guidelines: exercise playfulness in upfront and cheerful ways. Even if you want to sulk, lace it with love. Take care to be playful in trusted or familiar contexts. The liberties work positively only in a climate of love. So make sure that you make your care and appreciation evident in spheres where it is due. Moreover, to speed up change and transformation, forgive sincerely and move-on wholeheartedly. Do not allow past prejudices to linger. Allow yourself and others a fresh start.

Playful exchange can help you to expand your boundaries. The critical nature of playful contact can make you question your likes and dislikes. For example, I remember jumping around the room shrieking at the sight of a lizard on the wall, and my father asked me what seemed to be an out-of-context question: "Are you a mosquito?"

"No," I said defensively, still gripped by my false fears.

He said laughingly, "If you aren't a mosquito, you aren't her dinner?"

His comment made me immediately realize my false fear and mistaken response. I was spotting competition, enmity, and problems where there were none. I am now playful with lizards!

Playfulness vis-à-vis your goals can increase your productivity. While stressed and serious attitudes can overwhelm you, playful stances release your stress. And that comfortable relationship with your goal makes you actually achieve it. So for, instance, if you are wanting to lose twenty pounds, then having a playful approach of losing just three pounds in the first month will be more sustainable than the ambitious goal of losing twenty right away. Likewise, I know someone who wants to quit meat for good but he uses a month-to-month approach to make the goal look easy and attainable. At the end of each, he tells himself "it's just one more month." And that makes him see his austerity has less severe. In fact, he's been off meat for over a year now, without really feeling that it's been so long!

Playful attitudes can keep your mind light even as you pursue big goals. As a corollary, you will wear your achievements lightly. Since your pursuit was playful and didn't seem such a big deal, you won't make a big deal of it.

Finally, with all the above strategic stances, your company and care will positively influence others and your environment. I offer some exercises to keep your creative manner robust. Try them out!

OUTLOOKS AND GAMES FOR YOUR GROWTH

The reflections and exercises here are classified under five groups. These are: *complementary*: helping you to balance the dualities of life; *co-existing*: helping you to manage the mixed bag of feelings in you and energies around you; *colorful*: helping you to explore your versatility and enable your vivacity; *chaotic*: helping you to take in your stride the diversity and uncertainty of life; and *calm*: helping you to tap into your inner resources of relaxation and renewal at all times. Each group emphasizes a different route to ushering well-being in our lives, but they are all interrelated as well.

GROUP I: COMPLEMENTARY

Larger Aim: to engage positively with the dualities of life

Chosen Theme: Bouquets and Brickbats

General Outlook: In Asian outlook, dualities aren't seen as opposites but as two ends of the same continuum. In fact, it is due to the tussle between the two poles that we understand what either means. Deepak Chopra suggests that the one end of the continuum enables us to "experience" the other.[19] In other words, till you've seen hell, you don't know what heaven is! So the dualistic extremes are playing a creative role in building your insight. You can enable their role all the more by having suitable attitudes.

For a more positive rapport with all dualities, treat them as a married pair. So in our chosen theme, if you see Madame Bouquets coming your way, be aware that Monsieur Brickbats can't be far behind. This female yogi-poet in medieval India, Lal Ded, looked it them in a related way. Given her unconventional living, she would receive both vicious attacks as well as veneration from different people. Her way to maintain her balance was to tie a knot on one side of her scarf each time someone praised her and then tie another knot on the other side every time someone insulted her. In due course, both sides balance out each other![20]

Knowing that, make the most of both opportunities by maintaining your balance. So if life is throwing brickbats at you—criticism from others, or a rough patch at work, or loss of wealth—use the opportunity to introspect with honesty and polish your performance. Imagine if you only received bouquets? You'd really get a distorted picture of your place in the world. It is the brickbats that check us, straighten us, make us more vigilant, and urge us to do things in better ways. So don't get disheartened or abandon your dream. Hold on to your faith in the universe. Assume responsibility for your situation, even if you can't see your fault. In India, we tend to say, "It's all my karma." Likewise, when it is bouquet time, surely inhale all the energy of praise, but engage your humility as well to avoid becoming arrogant. Thus, bouquets will justly encourage you and brickbats will optimally train you.

A Sample Game: "Visual Morphing." Remember that "Black or White" video by Michael Jackson, where different men and women kept morphing into one another? We borrow from that technique here to help you take a balanced view of pleasant and unpleasant feelings/ events in your life.

Visualize two images, one negative and one positive. Make the negative one into a symbol of all the bothersome forces, like hurts and regrets. Choose a positive metaphor for all the blessings that you can think of in your life. Let's say you visualize a thorn for all the painful moments and a flower for all the prized ones. Behold real pictures of flower/thorn to visualize better.

Now sit on the floor (or on a chair) with your back supported. Take a few deep breaths and close your eyes. Now, upon each inhalation absorb the positive image, and upon each exhalation release the negative image. Do so for ten rounds. Even doing this much is a great healing exercise.

To take it further, let the images morph into one another. Morph the flower into the thorn and then morph the thorn into the flower. Maintain a steady pace of breathing. Your mind will be less affected by the polarities and in fact enhance its modularity.

Another game in the same group is *"Alter Ego and Devil's Advocate."* The devil's advocate criticizes while the alter ego supports. You can have your two siblings or young cousins posing as either! The aim of this game is to help you to refine your decision-making process. The devil's advocate is a deliberate disruptor, like this politician in this popular joke. Enjoy!

A conversation between an opposition leader and his secretary:

Secretary: *Sir, I just got news that the ruling party minister is making a visit to the flood-ridden village. We should we say to criticize?*

Politician: *Is he flying there or taking the train?*

Secretary: *What if he is flying, sir?*

Politician: *Well, then tell the villagers how spoiled the minister is! He is squandering taxpayers' money on expensive air travel when he can use all that money to help the villagers.*

Secretary: *Right, sir. But what if he is taking the train?*

Politician: *Well then tell the villagers how casual and insensitive the minister is. He is saving money on air travel just when the people need his timely help!*

GROUP II: CO-EXISTING

Larger Aim: To develop approaches for creative management of inner and outer diversity.

Chosen Theme: Competitiveness and Collaboration

General Outlook: Any mixture is a creative resource. Provided you can accept, and even expect the coexistence of positive and negative energies in everyone. They're in you as well. You can be smiling sincerely at one moment and smirking sarcastically at another. The moment you can accept this co-existence of good and bad as a fact of life and relationships, you will become more tolerant and less reactive. And that is what will make you release the creative potential innate in different mixtures.

Even in your better relationships, you will find the co-existence of a range of feelings. To take our chosen theme, you will find that your sibling is rather supportive but can also be quite competitive. Ditto for you! But instead of getting upset at the news, just accept it and remain conscious of it. Use this awareness strategically in order to serve the larger aims of fostering inspiration and integration.

Moreover, a thing in itself is not bad. It depends on how one uses it or what one takes from it. It is the same with envy and competitiveness. You can use it as a force to energize your performance. Like chess champion for years, Garry Kasparov, says: "We all work harder, run faster when we know someone is right on our heels."[21] So use the force of competitive feelings in you to work harder and outdo yourself.

Indeed, rising above your envy is indeed desire. For it motivates you to have collaborative and cooperative stances. Charles Darwin observed that in the animal and human world, those who collaborated built more sustainable systems for survival. Collaboration is better for your well-being too. A study finds that it reduces "personal insecurity" that accrues from "expectations of hostility from others."[22]

Even in the world of business, where one only imagines aggressive and competitive behavior, successful leaders know better. They know that the way to consumers' hearts are values that communicate care and cohesion. Project leaders know that the way to implement work is through successful involvement of people. Findings also suggest that all of us ultimately value "fairness over profit maximization,"[23] and are willing to make choices so that "everyone can be better off." And contrary to the instinctive feel we might have about this, studies tell us "a manufacturer and a retailer can both end up making more money if they are fair-minded (…) as opposed to merely maximizing their individual profits."[24]

Given the above benefits, we need ways to feel connected even in a climate of competition.

A Sample Game: "Tug of war." In the ordinary tug-of-war game, the winner is one who gets the better of the other. Here the winning side is one that ends up being better in terms of creativity and sensitivity! Just taking the goalpost higher!

This game is inspired from an episode in a play[25] (see note). Our aim is to compete here in a constructive and non-violent way. You can play this game with about ten children/teenagers at school or at a hobby center. (Youngsters are just more game for these kind of things!) Make the tug object not just any rope, but let's say one that is created out of tying many scarves end-to-end, each of which belongs to someone in the group. They will then be concerned with the well-being of the object as they wield it. So if you are tugging at your mom's scarf, you will be mindful of not jerking it in a way that tears it apart. Your concern will make you find a gentler way of using it.

In one group that did this exercise, one side began to create a graceful dance with the scarves, confusing the other side into relaxing their hold over the scarf-string. The competing side was caught unawares by this out-of-the-box thinking! Yet, given the playful means and creative aims of the game, there was hardly any streak of bitterness in the losing side. They were inspired instead to give a better out-of-the-box answer in the next round!

GROUP III: COLORFUL

Larger Aim: to enrich the palette of your and possibilities and your versatility

Chosen Theme: Major and Minor

General Outlook: Majors and minors in colleges are intended to be an interaction of key research areas with peripheral ones, both informing one another in exciting ways. Perhaps that's why, at top American universities, students are free to choose a large number of minors, even unlikely ones. At MIT, for example, engineering students choose from the drama and music as minors! Regular interaction with the arts helps these MIT "intellectuals" become more embodied in their thinking and their research methodologies benefit from the artistic approaches of openness, exploration, and flexibility.[26]

Each one of you has some dominant or major vocation. A student has studies as a major area, while a store-keeper has the task of running the store. However, as time passes, we become all too familiar with our major domain. And that makes us lose interest! A student who studies the same subjects in the same way actually becomes less receptive over a period of time, or the shopkeeper who favors the same routine becomes mechanical. Regular forays into of minor areas of interest will then energize your interest and improve your acumen in your major area. I know of a school principal that ensures that her students spend time in extra-curricular activities, despite parents being nervous about these minor activities. Her conviction, from years of experience, is that nothing drives up students' grades in core subjects more than this strategy!

Likewise, you may be a CEO who is looking at ways to enhance reach and profitability. Why not look at minor areas that you wouldn't look at traditionally? For example, some of the large paper companies today are looking at reforestation projects, because that tells the community that you don't just care about your profits but also about your environment and the lives of people.

Or you could be a model, a part of an environment where there is a lot of stress (pun in place!) over how you look and how others see you. That makes you sleepless over that extra inch around your waist or you feel guilty about the ice cream you ate or you tend to check your make-up every five minutes. Given the influence of your major milieu, looking after your looks has become the be all and end all. Give yourself a break! Look out for activities that make you think about your inner fitness as well. These minors will help you place your major focus in truer perspective. So you'll still be careful about your calories, but not obsessive. Your inner fitness regime will even add glow and warmth to your eyes. And the mascara will look nicer!

Moreover, doing things that we do not ordinarily do fans our flexibility too. As children, we would often do *seva* or community service. We would clean the dishes, mop the floors, and serve food to others. For us, it was akin to playtime and time-off from homework. But accompanying us would also be people in high places and ranks volunteering humbly for the same jobs that were seemingly beneath their position. Indeed, such a switch of stance can make you see your world with a new set of eyes. In this case, the minor activity necessitated that instead of expecting others to serve oneself; one would be on the lookout for opportunities to serve others. Evidently, with such experiences in other realms, we return to our own domain with a greater questioning of the meaning and purpose of our chosen domain. By doing what we do not do, we can give a conscious direction to what we do.

A minor area of interest does for a major what improvisation does for a set pattern. It improves, informs, enriches, and energizes. Sometimes it even creates new majors! For instance, gas stations on highways in the United States opened grocery outlets and restaurants so as to have their customers stop to shop and eat as well. Today, 95 percent of the revenues of gas stations come from this side business! Likewise what begins as a minor interest in your life could also mature into a major source of happiness one day.

Eventually, you will re-invent yourself as a result of a constant to and fro between your areas of focus and fancy. I am often asked how much emphasis should one place on a minor vis-à-vis a major. They also wonder if the distraction of the minor interest will reduce their concentration and focus on their major subject. Now, the alternation between the major and minor poles is necessary for the enrichment of either and for your evolution. Knowing that, you are the one who needs to set the rhythm of this to and fro. Just have broad structures of time-management and place conscious, albeit flexible limits on how much you do of one thing. So let's say if you've spend three hours working on your painting, you can surely spend the next couple of hours meeting people or listening to music. However, at another moment, you might feel like staying on your painting for a whole week before you decide to do something else over the weekend. Sometimes listen to your feelings and sometimes drag yourself to work even if you don't feel like it!

A Sample Game: "Just Major—No Minor." Actually the aim of this one is to take off the burden of the minor roles we impose on our relationships! In expecting others to deliver us everything, we scatter their energies and prevent them from playing the more important roles in our life. So, identify a major role played by someone in your life. Let's take the case of your mother. Look at your major expectation from her or what you like or enjoy most with her. Perhaps it is the great emotional support that she gives you. So you can articulate the major role as "great support" (not to be confused with "great sport"!). Now, for a week, you are to remain aware of this major role. (Use visual reminders.) Also, at any point if you get bothered about something she did or said, recall the major role you've assigned to her and remain focused on that. So if she is telling you that you should change into another dress because this one is too provocative (or another tie because she find the current one too jarring), then persuade her playfully to see your point of view or accommodate hers. Whatever you do, just remain mindful that she is your great support and you aren't going to do or say anything that creates a wall between you and your great support. And if you want compliments for your tie or dress, fulfill that minor need elsewhere! Ask someone who will be polite, and not blunt like your mom.

By focusing on the more important roles of your core relationships, you'll in fact strengthen those roles in them. So the more you see your mother as a support and respond to her with that awareness, the more of a support she will become—and perhaps due to that a great sport too!

When you want 100 percent from someone, you don't even enjoy the 50 percent you get. And because of your unhappy receiving, you'll begin to devalue what you have as well. Yet, if you can focus on the 50 percent that you do get and receive it with thankfulness, then your response and behavior will stimulate the other as to give you more that he or she currently does. Also, if you focus on your major needs, you'll naturally rationalize your real needs as well. The 50 percent that you get will actually begin to feel as good as the 100 percent! Thus focusing on the major role of the other will exert an uplifting force on your relationship and a correcting force on your expectations. You will cherish what you have and thus make the most of it.

GROUP IV: CHAOTIC

Larger Aim: managing inner and outer chaos

Chosen Theme: Boundaries and Bridges

General Outlook: Boundaries enable us stay on our independent course, bumping least into others, while bridges enable us to connect positively and sensitively with our society and environment. Lack of boundaries will give rise to excessive intrusion while lack of bridges will drive up indifference. Balance!

Now when we drive on the road, the boundaries of lane driving, speed limits, traffic signals, etc., ensure that we don't keep running into one another or block one another's path. In life, too, you need boundaries or rules of conduct in order to ensure smooth and sustainable co-existence among a diverse group. Sometimes the boundaries are evident, but more often than not you need to figure them out.

By becoming conscious of your boundaries or limits, you can prevent yourself from intruding upon the well-being of others and your environment. So curtail your freedom through exercising self-restraint, placing suitable limits on your consumption and expression, and bearing respectful conduct toward one and all.

To place limit on your consumption, adopt the path of least intrusion. Take lessons from the tiger that despite being strong enough to feed on everyone if he likes does not feed on everything all the time. He only hunts when hungry. He takes what he needs and stops when he doesn't. Not us!

As we all know, in our day-to-day actions, we are acting in over-the-top ways without even realizing that we are tipping the delicate balances in our environment. For example, in your simple act of buying food beyond your needs, this is what is further set into motion —producers are obliged to make more, thus increasing demand for ingredients and also inputs like electricity, machinery, packing material, and transport. There is evidently more pollution generated throughout the processes adding its bit to global warming, which further leads to flooding, drought, depletion of the ozone layer, and exposure to hazardous UV rays. These affect your health, raise your medical bills, hamper your work and relationships, and adversely impact your well-being and happiness.

In short, every time you consume in uncaring and unconscious ways, there is a lot of pressure that you place on your well-being at all levels, without even realizing it.

So ask yourself every time you shower or drive: can you expend less? A good rule of thumb is to take no more than you need, and give no less than you can. Also, choose your limits in the light of do-ability— so if your office is fifteen miles away, walking up till there will leave you exhausted and stressed at work. So don't be foolhardy. Just be questioning and conscious about where you can save and where must you spend.

Contrary to what you may feel about this, boundaries do not limit you. They actually multiply your potential. Take the case of a piece of land. Now if you simply erect four walls on it, you get one big hall. But if you consciously place limits and boundaries within it, you create many more rooms and can assign different purposes to them (for individual study, social interactions et al). So just like structuring a house makes you use an otherwise undifferentiated resource in versatile ways, in the same way managing your many energies through self-discipline and self-management will make you accomplish so much more by pressing into action your different dimensions.

Also, you need to keep earning, or engaging, or giving back. These 'bridges' of connecting to your environment will balance the shortfall created through your intrusion and also counter your indifference.

Sharing is another vital way to redistribute resources. In India, there are conscious practices of returning to society through sharing your wealth. Some businesses even have god and goddesses as their "partners"! They set aside his or her fair share of profits, which is then used for philanthropic purposes. But you can also share and transmit insights, knowledge, wisdom, love, laughter and trust. These are the real resources that drive material growth.

A Sample Game: "So what do I really want?" This game will help you to see where you'd like to invest your time and energy and where you'd like to save them. It will help you evaluate and revisit your priorities. And just that can set many things right!

Quickly get a piece of paper, a pencil, and an eraser! Jot down, from the top of your mind, ten things that you want from your life. Randomly, the list could look like this.

1. Happiness and peace of mind
2. Being loved and well-being
3. Good health

4. Lots of money
5. Loving spouse/children and their happiness
6. Power and position in job
7. Nice house
8. Lovely holidays
9. Good education
10. Good workplace

Take another look (at your own list) to make sure that you haven't missed out on other things you value. Now, place these ten desires in order of priority. I will use the above list as my reference.

Of course, you'd ideally like to have all your ten wishes fulfilled. However, we don't always get all that we want. We are constantly required to make choices and trade-offs. So in this game, to really know if your priorities are in the order that you have placed them in, ask yourself this: let's say, to meet your priority four, would you be willing to (if required) to give up, say, priority nine? If your answer is 'no', then it means that your priority number nine is in effect more important than you currently think. So reorganize your priorities at this point. (Verify similarly for other priorities as well.)

Now especially as you will come up to the top five priorities, the choices will begin to look really tough. So, in the given example, ask yourself if you are, for instance, willing to give up priority five—loving spouse/children and their happiness—for lots of money in priority four? "What kind of question is that!" you might exclaim. But make these choices nonetheless; just to know for yourself the real value of different aspects of your life. Also, this is not a onetime exercise. You can redo this exercise once every few weeks. It's okay to have a change of priorities!

So currently, if you do value 'four' over 'five', then you will beget inner clarity to give priority to that lucrative job offer, and so become more accepting of the fact that you will have to live away from family for months at a stretch.

Life is all about the choices you make and happily living with them. Happiness emerges from clarity, not confusion. So make this game your vital companion to clear up confusion in different spheres of your life.

Another game: "Trade-Offable": This is a sister exercise to the one above, and more instant in its effect. Try this—if something in your current situation is bothering you and you are unable to accept it, and then imagine a conference with the universal giver, who is willing to give you anything in return for your acceptance. So let's say you are unable to accept that you are unemployed currently. Now imagine the universal giver giving you the option of asking for anything else that would make you so happy that you gladly accept your bitter reality. So let's say a free Mediterranean cruise will really perk your spirits and help you to accept your situation. Now the moment you say aha to the new option, you will have an important realization—that your desires are actually trade-offable!

Whether you get the cruise or not is not the point. The point is that given a twist in the tale, you actually became happy with the same situation that was making you miserable a moment ago. The sheer realization that you can actually trade-off one wish for another is quite liberating! There's also that chance that the universe will reward you for your acceptance by granting you your bartered wish. So why curse the universe when you can charm it!

GROUP V: CALM

Larger Aim: To rest, be rejuvenated, and renew your commitment to a positive life.

Chosen Theme: Harmony and Healing

General Outlook: Life rocks you every day. You face ups and downs at work, in relationships and in your personal consciousness. To make positive use of all your inner questions and dilemmas, you need to come back to them with a fresh mind and free spirit. You thus need regular recourse to activities that enable your calm and composure. The moments of calm and carefree observation are hardly 'wasted'. They help you to review and renew yourself.

Various relaxation techniques can induce steadiness in your breath and thus mind. Natalie Goldberg, painter, artist, and writer, considers stress to be nothing but a "forgetting of the breath."[27]

Here is a way to reconnect to your relaxed breath and by that awaken an inner state of prayer, wherein negative blocks are naturally dissolved and positive energies intensify.

A Sample Game: "State of prayer": In a dimly lit comfortable place, play a piece of soothing music. Lie on the floor in the classic corpse pose—a posture of utter surrender. Relax fully. Feel your body sinking into the ground. Let go of all kinds of thoughts. Visualize a bright golden light (or white or blue, depends on your response to the color) enveloping and nourishing you. After fifteen minutes, or when you feel fully rested, prepare to come back to your ordinary rhythms of life. But return gently. Keep your eyes closed for a while. Arise into a comfortable sitting position. Fold your hands, straighten your back and expand your chest. Inhale your world afresh. In this privileged state, you might yourself praying or saying things in a way that you rarely do otherwise. It's your liberated self-speaking. Listen to it.

Another game: "Stand and Stare": Counter your constant busyness by doing 'nothing' for a change. Take a stroll in a park, or look at the plants in your garden, or watch children play on the street. Notice the "squirrels hide their nuts in grass," as W.H. Davies wrote in his poem "Leisure."

Take this opportunity to observe nature as if under a microscope, patch by patch. You will see miracles in every blade of grass. The other day as I was walking, I saw a stream of ants carrying together some grains of rice. And then the cleaning lady arrived. In one swish of her broom, she brushed all their hard work aside! "Poor things," I muttered.

Yet, the behavior of the ants gave no evidence of them being poor things! They were tenacious little things that were right back on track, carrying the grains of rice yet again! For me personally, that was a day when I was exhausted and had almost given up on my efforts (of editing this book!). Observing the ant antics, I too was energized to try again.

THE FINISH LINE

Equipped with suitable approaches, you will relate in creative ways with life's diversity and will not become panicked and perplexed by it. In any case, you will now be less prone to expressing egoistically, behaving aggressively, and reacting disproportionately. You will thus be making space for the emergence of something more vital within you—your truer voice.

Voice is identity, a sense of self, a sense of relationship to others, and a sense of purpose. Voice is power—power to express ideas and connections, power to direct and shape an individual life towards a productive and positive fulfillment for self, family, community, nation, and the world.
Beverly McElroy-Johnson[28]

CHAPTER 6
CREATIVE VOICE—
ENERGIZE YOUR PART AND PLAY

Voice, as used here, is about having conscious mechanisms and means to express and engage in fuller ways. I offer here four pillars upon which to rest and test your feelings and reflections, so that your interpersonal context leaves you strengthened in every way.

Cultivating a *considered voice* will make you receive and express views with criticality yet care. Consulting your *conscientious voice* will make you refer periodically to your inner voice and in turn be prompted more often by it. Engaging in a *creative vocation (voice)* will stimulate your seeking spirit and shape your independent insight. Finally, all these clearer voices, variously energizing your mind and manner, will uplift your *collaborative voice*, or your dynamism to get along with different people and make them get along among themselves. You will thus become better at managing your interpersonal reality and using its various opportunities. Your emergent well-being and wisdom will uplift your creativity all the more.

YOUR CONSIDERED VOICE: HARD LOOKS, SOFT TONES

Your considered voice is a balanced blend of your critical regard and your caring heart. Dialogue, debate, and deliberation develop your critical voice, as Amartya Sen calls it.[29] On the other hand, a caring voice is essential to maintain your sense of connection with the other even as you have a different point of view. Unchecked by your caring voice, your critical voice can become dominating, aggressive and hurtful. Invoking your caring voice will keep your empathy simmering, and so your difference of opinions will not divide you from others.

Groom your critical voice by consciously listening to others. A student once told me that she fared much better in classes where she had a friend to talk to after the lecture was over. In discussing she would discover so many new facets of the subject at hand.

Every one knows something that you don't. So ask questions. Become curious. You will also reconsider your half-baked opinions and interrogate your assumptions. Alternate voices will exert a corrective and enriching influence on your voice.

Also, you can learn so much more about the sensibilities of other people by asking their opinions. You can learn so much about the state of humanity by listening to the stories and experiences of others.

Ordinarily, we become defensive and want to win arguments. In doing so, we let go of the creative opportunity of critical contact. To make the most of it, prefer to put across your opinions in positive and playful ways. Avoid aggressive gestures and stay positively passionate. When you wish to be critical of another's point, make it fair and fun. Question yourself too as you question others. Admit your own mistakes too and not just point out the flaws in others. Instead of panicking in the wake of questions that you cannot answer, use it as in opportunity to polish your understanding. It is good when you don't have answers on the tip of your tongue. Because then you can go deeper in search for them.

When discussing someone else's limitations, do so with an attitude that another's limitation is just a variant of yours. For example, you may observe another person to be miserly. Instead of quickly judging, use the opportunity to reconsider and review your own measured stances toward giving. You can tell yourself that since you do not like such behavior in others, you will reduce such tendencies in yourself as well. Moreover, use your observations to strengthen your vigilant thinking. If you know of the troubled zones in others, then steer clear of the trouble!

Whenever you want to talk about the matter, do so in a playful spirit. You can also talk about instances where you faced a similar problem and how you learnt your lessons. This will put the other person at ease, as he or she will not feel singled out for reproach. Take care not to hurt the other. See this person as your own mother or daughter: the patience and warmth will come. In fact, when the latter are present, the other person will even take your tough comments in the right spirit. So create the bond first.

To prevent critical exchanges from turning sour, you need to take the help of your caring and serving voice, which is your very soul nature. While criticality stimulates our heads, caring for others invokes our hearts and theirs. Just channel the heat of the head into the warmth of the heart, and you'll find that disagreements will not become disagreeable. Now our different heads can be full of different things, but our hearts long for the same things: warmth, care and respect. Serve this longing of the other. So readily make a cup of coffee for your friend to melt away the rising defenses.

Importantly, when you wish to cultivate a shared vision (as in a family or team), encourage all to express their independent views. Through stimulating the voices of your friends and family members, you stand to benefit most from their support in the long run. In fact, you should play a generous role in backing them, including assuming their mistakes. In doing so, you will free them of their fears and act with empowerment. In return for your generous stance, you will beget their loyalty and unshakeable support. But don't expect it!

Enable your group to engage in "parallel thinking," as Edward De Bono calls it. This means telling all to look at a common direction at a given moment and optimally explore a subject. This will reduce noisy and distracting cross talk and curb egoistic compulsions to contradict others. When you want some in the group to play devil's advocates, announce your strategy. That will ensure that those who are playing the opposition are not seen as devils by the rest!

Finally, as an Indian proverb says, you must learn from all, but at the end of it all, go by the counsel of your inner voice. Let's see how we can listen to it.

YOUR CONSCIENTIOUS VOICE: STRENGTHENING YOUR SPIRIT

While the caring voice connects you to the winsomeness of your heart, your conscientious voice connects you to its wisdom. You can ignore what others say, but bend backward to hear and follow your inner voice.

Your heart is your soul in action. Your heart is happiest and most uplifted when it feels true to your soul nature—expansive, joyous, fair, and peaceful. Your conscience is the voice of your soul and can be heart if you open the doors of your heart.

Your conscience is a far more expansive consciousness than your ordinary awareness. When you invoke its advice, in a relaxed and seeking state of mind, it will give you small yet significant pointers toward improving your act. It can see things that you miss or spin. It can call a spade a spade. It is your inner force of correction and evolution. Don't live without it!

When asking your conscience for advice, ask with honesty and simplicity. Frame simple questions like, "Dear heart (dear conscience sounds intimidating!), do you feel good after what I just did?" or, "Dear heart, would you feel better if I take a positive action instead of feeling bad and complaining?" You will find that the promptings of your conscience are surprisingly simple and guileless. When in tune with it, you won't go rambling into lengthy analysis. You will simply say a 'yes' or a 'no,' shake your head or nod in agreement. Now just act upon it!

You can also invoke the voice of your conscience by simply recalling your larger purpose. The way this security guard did. Posted outside the Intensive Care Unit (ICU) of a hospital in New Delhi, he was being badgered by relatives of patients to be allowed entry to the ICU beyond the visiting hours. When the hardy guard didn't relent, one of the visitors snapped: "Thank you so much for not letting me meet my dying brother." Other bystanders backed his sarcastic offensive and even supported it with their nasty mutterings and glances. The guard then spoke to explain his stance. He said: "Dear visitors, my prime duty is to ensure that your relation, and our patient, comes out of this door feeling healthier and better than when he or she came in. I am doing everything to ensure that we all meet that desired goal. I also, therefore, must not do a few things that might stand in our way. This includes not letting you in at a time when the patients are resting. So even though I am not helping you right now, in doing so I am truly helping you. I hope you understand." They did.

With mindfulness of your greater purpose, which includes the bigger picture, you naturally make choices with due diligence. Take this example, where you set your larger purpose or Dharma, as we say in India, at "excelling in your studies." Now you will need to make certain choices to realize your aim. These would include studying for eight hours a day (at least!), read avidly, take part in group discussions et al. But since all work and no play will dull your mind, you also need to take out time for sporty activities and hobbies to relax and energize. To keep your mind strong, you will need to cultivate positive thoughts so as to overcome performance anxiety or fear of failure. You will need to eat nutritious food and also exercise for maintaining your health and fitness. Then, you'd much rather avoid getting into fights with other people, as having a police record or landing in a hospital would make the going even tougher for you. You also need to work for harmony at home in order to feel secure and supported. And so on... As you can see, the mere mindfulness of your overarching (positive) purpose will help you make optimal choices in different quarters of your life.

In the film *Glory Road* (2006), there is this episode where the team is demoralized as a result of the mounting racial attacks. Given the stress, they all start fighting among themselves! Seeing this, a man on the team quips that they all are forgetting their real purpose, which is to win the championship. So are we in our lives.

Now whenever you are catching a flight or boarding a train, aren't you mindful of where you are headed. And even when you take a detour for a snack or making a phone call, you remain just as conscious. Develop the same concentration on your greater goal in daily life too. And when you feed in your destination or greater purpose in the GPS (Global Positioning System) of your conscience, it will keep prompting you about the viable routes. It will also tell you where you took a wrong turn and how you can get back on track. Your conscience is really your best friend.

Importantly, so as to not confuse your inner voice with the cross talk of your ego and its biases, you need to consult it when you have a cool head, warm heart and an honest regard. Normally, that which warms the heart naturally cools the head and makes way for honesty. So put the heart first. Awaken its force through prayer, mind games for empathy, or a stance of helpfulness and service.

Indeed, in silence, and better still in prayer, you will engage more actively with your conscience. In prayer, you are open to hear the answers as they come. Also, given that you are seeking solace for yourself, you are also readier to forgive others. Likewise, in serving others—through small gestures and hearty goodwill– you will tend to think and act with concern, fairness and balance. However, in case of conflict between your well-being and another's, serve yourself first! So if your conscience tells you to make-up with someone but you don't have the energy for it, please take rest! Even in a flight, the hostess asks you to wear your own oxygen mask before you can help another. So stabilize yourself before you stretch yourself.

Eventually, your conscience is telling you how to balance your actions. Now sometimes we bring misery because of excessive intervention and sometimes due to deficient response and action. If you are the shy, reticent, and deficient-in-action type, ask yourself what you would have done had a certain incident transpired with your child or parent. You will free your conscience from the burden of your fears and thus normalize it. On the other hand, if you are already over-confident and aggressive, ask yourself what you would do if the perpetrator or provocateur in your situation were your own daughter or mother. You will free your conscience from the burden of anger and thus normalize it.

On the same subject, someone once told me that you only feel bad about something when you are not letting your conscience stand up for what you know deep down is right for you—that which is in sync with your own values.

When you live by your values, it will touch a chord with others too. There is this Indian story of a Sikh disciple who took upon himself to serve water to all the wounded soldiers in the battlefield, including those from the enemy camp. The Sikhs soldiers complained to their guru about this man from in effect their own community who was helping the enemy. Upon being summoned by the guru, this man was asked to explain his behavior. In his defense, he gave his reasons as such: "I am serving all because I see god in all. This is what you have always taught me. And this is what I am applying in my life." The guru was very pleased that this man was not just saying the right thing but had fully imbibed the teachings and was able to apply them even in a challenging situation. He allowed him to continue his compassionate work and even urged him to give first aid to the wounded.

Conscientious thinking thus coaxes your true voice—where there is no room for fear and only a true sense of purpose. And that has an uplifting effect on everyone. To make your conscience flow liberally and freely at all times, you need to create a special channel for it. That's why you need a creative vocation.

YOUR CREATIVE-VOCATION VOICE: EXPLORING YOUR BETTER SELF

Every seed in nature is meant to sprout. You too are a seed of nature. In the company of your creative muse, your inner and finer reality will steadily sprout and assume its veritable form. Your outward personality and inner potential will begin to integrate. And you will feel more integrity in yourself.

Your creative vocation is your dedicated space where you can dump your doubts and clear them as well. It will get you into the habit of talking to your conscience every day. Now an Indian proverb says that when you give someone an inch, he or she will take a mile! The conscience is no different! Give it a little room and it will begin to invade your mental space in no time. In due course, it will start following you and prompting you wherever you go.

Your creative vocation will enable you to digest your diverse influences and feelings in constructive ways. It is a fascinating site of contact between your existing and possible self. With it, you will begin to take active part in the process of creation, rejection and transformation of your own thoughts. Of course, watching a creative product evolve with your labor and love is hugely satisfying as well. Then, as your achievements become visible to you, you will gain in confidence. As they become visible to others, you will be heard and respected more. Add the weight of performance to your voice, not the weight of your ego!

Therefore, you need to have personal creative goals like composing music or designing objects etc. A graduate student once told me that she understood a subject much better when she wrote papers instead of appearing for tests. She said that the process of exploring and elaborating a paper over a period of time made her feel more intimate and integrated with her subject. As she lived longer with her subject, its lessons lingered more in her mind.

You'll notice that whenever you are engaged in a creative vocation, you beget a more seeking spirit in your ordinary interactions too. You move around with greater witnessing, sensitivity and reflection and thus come home with some food for thought. Even when commit yourself to a simple task like creating a collage or collection of inspirational stories for yourself, you will become so much more oriented to spotting goodness in others. You will start becoming more aware of all that is inspirational in your environment. Also, with a creative task occupying your imagination, you will have little energy to expend on ego games or negative thinking. You'll have your hands and minds full!

Significantly, you develop the mental habits of watching, questioning, exploring, elaborating, streamlining, structuring and coming to your own conclusions. These habits then seep into other spheres of your life, resulting in greater awareness therein too.

Moreover, when you find strength in your own positive pursuits, you will automatically avoid the negative route of feeling stronger by making others feel weaker or inferior. You will learn that true confidence, true pride, and true security are earned through integrity and hard work. And they leave you with a longer lasting high, unlike the momentary release that you get by using ego or pressure tactics to look superior.

In your creative vocation, you get the sacred liberty of experimenting, exploring, and proposing with a freer imagination, unlike in the sphere of interpersonal relations where you need to be conscious of your conduct, as it affects others. On the creative route thus, you can develop your independent approaches quicker and sans fear. In real life, the quick moves of proposing, changing and challenging can cause anxiety and confusion. Just try this exercise. Instruct your friend like this: "Turn left. No, right. Actually, straight is better. Hey, we can try that other route!" Your friend will most likely turn around and ask you to make up your mind!" This is exactly what you are doing on the route of creative exploration! But here, instead of getting stressed or stressing others, you are enjoying the circuitous and uncertain journey. Making room for this kind of exploration is essential to develop your thinking. It energizes your ability to link up ideas in non-linear ways. The creative process thus gives a great workout to your imagination and gears it for innovative thinking.

But how do you find suitable creative vocations? Should you follow a given opportunity? Or should you create one that you fancy? Well, there are no standard routes. But there is a standard technique—keep courting new ideas. You'll soon know whether you want to commit to them or not!

Your creative activities will gradually become like green signals in your life. The moment you work on them or merely think of them, you will be infused with a positive energy to forge ahead. This green signal will remind you that you need to move onward and justly overcome the obstacles en route. Now, when driving on the road, if someone starts a fight with you, won't you positive response if you need to reach your office on time? Likewise, the mere thought of your creative vocation will uplift you and make you deal with your present with patience. Your creative world will become your greater reality.

Author Sheila Weinstein confirms: "*If I stay connected to my (creative) work, I stay unafraid. My inner life is my real life. It feeds me constantly and renews me. I find that I can cope with what arises in my outer reality because my creative work provides me with my true center."*[30]

Revisit your green signal often, at least for a couple of hours in a day, even if not at stretch. Even the scattered visitations, let's say taking fifteen minutes off from your lunchtime or waking up an hour earlier in the mornings, will energize you amply. Make a start, however imperfect it seems. Even your small steps will take you somewhere. And again, the process is the key part. The product is only a carrot to keep you going!

Importantly, maintain a constant to and fro between your creative realm and your real life. Let your inspired thoughts uplift your daily life, and in turn allow your ordinary interactions to interrogate your inspiration. So for instance, I often read my own book for guidance in my real life, and in turn I use my real situations to poke and question my motivated thoughts. Normally, people complain that wise thoughts are bookish and not 'practical.' This mode of to and fro will precisely help you to apply your own better thoughts, in your own way, to your own life.

Eventually, when this inner-outer interaction reaches its acme, you will find inspiration coming to you of its own accord. Thoughts will erupt spontaneously, ideas will come together magically, and eureka moments will be aplenty. The speeding up of any process leads to the release of a new consciousness. So keep working at your creative activity bit by bit. One day, it will flower. Along with it, you will too.

There are peculiar challenges to be faced upon your creative journey though. There will be moments when you will feel tired and exhausted. At many points of writing this book, I would often get into self-doubting modes. "My God, who's going to ever read all of this?" However, I learned quickly that while reflection adds, anxiety depletes. An Indian saint-poet has said that worries reduce the radiance on your face and the force of your intelligence. In any case, the very purpose of any creative vocation is to liberate your mind. So don't lock it in fear or arrogance. Adopt suitable outlooks to allay your anxieties.

Indian thought offers a helpful approach. It urges you to look at yourself as a receptive instrument of a higher creative force, instead of seeing yourself as the ultimate creator. Such an attitude allows you to create with more abandon. Seeing yourself as a small but significant player in the larger scheme of the universe will make you feel at once stronger and humble. Your strength will give you solidity while your humility will give you porosity. You need both.

Author Elizabeth Gilbert likewise urges you to strike a partnership between the creative spirit and your own work on a creative project (in her case, it is her writing). She says your job is to "just show up"[31] and expect the creative spirit to show up as well! Also, since the real author/doer/creator isn't you but this invisible creative spirit, then evidently the failure belongs to it, and so do the successes. Such a stance is Vedantic too—just do your duty and leave the rest to the caring and conscious energy we call God. Then, if you succeed, you will have gratitude. If you fail, you won't lose faith.

Whenever anxiety begins to mount and gets the better of you, just drop your creative agenda for a while and pursue other things—go for a stroll, watch a film, or invite your friends over. You'll return to your muse with gusto.

The final aspect of your fuller voice is your ability to harness the creative force flowing in others through your active stance of collaboration. To collaborate successfully, you need to develop inner security to not feel threatened; generosity to give others their due in terms of space and credits; and humility to receive and learn from others in a genuine way.

YOUR COLLABORATIVE VOICE: STIMULATING OTHERS WITH YOUR BETTER NATURE

In India, we say that when one person comes together with another one, they don't make a two—they make an eleven! You attain goals faster, and in a much fuller way, with people lending you helping hands at a variety of levels. Jack Welch, the dynamic leader of General Electric, confirms: "Change agents are not Lone Ranger types. Quite the contrary; the most effective change agents always have a strong core of supporters."[32]

Be it in business, sport or life, cooperation is a winning strategy. All you need to curb is your ego and favor transparency and truth. Getting started might seem difficult. But soon you will realize that being connected and in harmony can really simplify your life and uplift your efforts.

But how can you feel this unity with others, given that visually, we are all so different from one another. Rise above the apparent reality of difference by focusing on our shared inner reality. Put yourself in the habit of seeing others with your "third eye". Our two eyes search for duality while our singular eye focuses on unity.

In Indian thought, our individual souls have the same nature; we are all full of love, joy, and peace within. "You can't be but love,"[33] says guru Sri Sri Ravishankar. So despite our distinct faces, fingerprints, and voices, we are all cosmic siblings.

Your caring voice opens the doors of your heart and allows you to see with the third eye of unity. Smiling, helpfulness, gratefulness, graciousness, and serving others, all enable you to feel a deep underlying connection with others, even strangers. To support this good start, uphold it by having prayers in your heart for the well-being of all, including your foes and competitors. And if they are happy, they'll let you be!

To strengthen your respect for others and see them as your better halves, think often of their great roles in enabling you to do what you are able to do. This businesswoman I know once compared her team at work to her car's wheels. "I roll because of them," she said. So will you!

Also, in depending on others and in delegating work to them, you divide your many sources of stresses and can focus single-mindedly on whatever you wish to

Of course, continuing and successful collaboration will require that you have the modesty and humility to share the credits. Ordinarily, we pat ourselves when we taste success and blame others when we fail. But this behavior will alienate others. As a thumb rule, acknowledge more than less, and take on more responsibility than due. Shoulder more and share more. That's a sure way to well-being and growth.

SING YOUR SONG!

Freed from your ego and connected to others, you will now beget a more authentic and just voice. However, do not be disheartened if others do not yet see things the way you do. As Nobel laureate Rabindranath Tagore wrote in a Bengali song, "If they don't answer your call, walk alone." If your call has the ring of truth and sincerity and is uplifting for all, it will surely find backers and takers in due course.

Yet, to create your songs and calls, you need a well-developed ear for harmony, which will deepen your sensitivity and intuitive understanding of your inner and outer worlds. Our final section is all about helping you listen well, combine well, and create well—the ways magicians and musicians do.

PART III: CREATING

Engaging Your Soul:
Harnessing The Power Of Sound
And Music

He who sings scares away his woes.
—Cervantes

CHAPTER 7

PLAYING IN YOUR VIBRATIONAL WORLD

In life, the many invisible forces far exceed our visible realities. Now your vision can help you to see better, provided there is light. But in its absence, your ears are a better guide. Since we are quite in the dark about who we are, what the other is and what the universe is all about, we need to hone our hearing in order to navigate better vis-à-vis ourselves, others and our environment.

It is said that when natural calamities are imminent, animals sense it much more and much earlier, as they live in tune with their environment. The intuitive capacity is precisely about this—where the intelligence of both thought and feeling converge. So with a better vision, the force of your thinking is sharpened. And with acute listening, you get a better 'feel' of the various forces within and around you. Just like seeing better enables your bigger picture thinking, sensitive hearing stands to empower your better sense.

In this section, you will understand how your aural environment affects you, and how you can influence it with the sounds and rhythms that you create via your thoughts, words, vibes, and responses. It will help you become more attuned to situations as they are, and importantly develop a harmoniously sensibility to manage and modify diverse energies in it. Having developed the musical modes of thinking and feeling, you will be motivated to uplift your given reality by suffusing it with your positive vision and direction.

In doing so, you will become an ally and extension of nature. It will then be eager to work through you.

YOUR VIBRATIONAL ECOSYSTEM

In many civilizations, sound is seen as the creative stimulus for our differentiated and dynamic universe. That also makes it a vehicle that can lead you back to the One. When you are aware on the underlying unity of all energy, then most matters seem similar to you, even when they have different details and traits.

Modern science and ancient intuition agree that from planets to people, we are all vibrating. You may not be able to hear it all, but all the same, the Earth sounds like a canary,[1] "mercury has a chirping, quick-silvery sound,"[2] this black hole emanates "a B flat."[3] Your cells, organs, genes and DNA too sing their own tunes, and your emotions have frequencies. Recent research (2007) also suggests that your nerves communicate using sound, not electricity.[4] Interestingly the Sanskrit name for nerves is *nadi*, meaning that which carries *nada*, or sound.

The cosmic dialogue is in the language of vibrations. Yet, only the harmonious interactions are favored and furthered by the universe.[5] As children of the universe, we too prefer the same. We instantly take to the harmonizing vibrations of care and love. We then feel reassured in the company of others and are more at peace within. We even prefer to buy objects that sound pleasant, just like we prefer to pick art that relaxes and soothes. Research suggests "product names with vowel sounds that convey positive attributes about the product are deemed more favorable by consumers."[6] Unlike sights that offer concrete pictures, sound is only suggestive of pictures. It thus works your imagination much more. Evidently, the influence of therapeutic sounds and harmonious patterns will uplift the way your imagination works. That's our aim!

Scientific experiments confirm that properties of objects begin to change when exposed to different sounds. It is well-known that plants respond positively to soothing music. One lady grows lusciously large dahlias and avows it's because she sings to them! Even inanimate and hardened objects, like metal, are susceptible to changes through sound, as scientist J.C Bose showed.[7] Then, human voice at certain frequencies has been found to dissolve cancer cells too.[8] Even in our daily interactions, you will observe that when someone speaks respectfully to you, your positive feelings strengthen, while when someone speaks angrily to you, your negative emotions surface. So we need to foremost become aware of the ways in which we are affected ourselves, and are affecting others, through the subtle play of vibrations.

Our deep responsiveness to sound has a physical basis as well. Music-therapist Barbara J. Crowe says that "our first awareness is auditory, and we process our world through sound for many months after birth."[9] Also, as we are primarily constituted of water— we are in effect fluid entities—so sound waves affect us even quicker.

By taking help from healing sounds, viz. mantra, music, and meditation (three Ms), you can alter your awareness through sharper and smarter listening, and creative transformation of your thoughts and emotions.

HOW MANTRAS, MUSIC, AND MEDITATION CAN WORK FOR YOU

MANTRAS

Audio awakens and re-directs your attention. Remember when your teacher would call out your name in the middle of her lecture? Your wandering attention would return! Interestingly, your brain has the property of traveling along any sound it is exposed to. That's the facility you make use of to distract your child's attention from any given tantrum.

Mantra yoga is a veritable path of changing and challenging the landscape of your mind through conscious sound combinations. While ordinary words can redirect your attention, mantra sounds can recreate your very awareness. "Mantra creates a new groove and the mind begins to spontaneously flow into the groove created by the mantra,"[10] says Swami Veda Bharati. So if you affirm a mantra that prays for the welfare of all, then all your emotional energies will converge toward this inclusive end.

The thought or content of the mantra uplifts your awareness, whereas its sonic energy affects your spirit in direct ways. Just like looking at certain colors stimulates you physiologically and psychologically, likewise, receiving certain sounds creates inner energy. It is for this reason that Swami Bhoomananda Tirtha says that reciting or listening to mantras are not merely "auditory processes."[11] They result in the very "churning of our consciousness." [12]

You can use mantras in different ways to initiate shifts of awareness. First, you could chant a chosen mantra (mindful of its meaning and import) as part of your meditation practice. In this heightened state of concentration, you integrate most with a mantra's energy. To partake of the mantra's sound energy, chant using your body as a resonator. Fill up your whole body with the sounds. The sounds will cleanse and recreate your inner world.

You can even use a musical note as a mantra. Just maintain steadiness and concentration during the toning. You will feel your scattered energies coming together and thus feel more collected. The physical benefits of chanting and humming include reduced stress and cholesterol, improved cardiac and respiratory functioning, and stronger immunity. It even keeps your sinuses clear!

Eventually, prefer a simple mantra that you can relate to. You can even use an ordinary word that means something special to you. Or you can use an affirmation that brings you cheer. So you could chant, "Thank god for everything," or repeat, "I can do it," or affirm, "I am so blessed." But do create positive alternatives!

A second approach is to repeat your mantras mechanically. This option isn't as bad as it sounds. It will at least keep your mind pegged to the anchor of the mantra and restrain its hyperactivity. Significantly, your mechanical habit will build your reflex to recall your mantras frequently, including in challenging situations. It will thus help you to stay calm in situations that catch you unawares.

A third way is a blend of the above two. In this case, you use the mantra as an accompaniment to your daily chores. So you liltingly chant while being involved in routine tasks like, packing your suitcase, cooking a meal, cleaning your room et al. When you add mantras to your ordinary tasks, the latter become meditative and relaxing. They feel more special and satisfying. Your repetitive drone will be a source of calm and comfort for you. And sometimes even for others. I was once chanting like this in a slightly audible tone at an airport. Minutes later, a lady standing behind me cooed in my ears: "It's really so nice to hear someone sing at baggage reclaim!" We briefly chatted and parted rather pleased with our positive contact.

Likewise, dedicating your mantras for the well-being of someone will make you chant with fullness of feeling. Dedication is a way to uplift any activity. Dedication is meditation in action.

Choose mantras to balance your energies. So don't use a mantra for more confidence if you are already over-confident! Traditionally, a guru, or an enlightened master would hand over a suitable mantra to a seeker, for he would have a broader vision of what the seeker needed to evolve. In general, if you are easy to anger, and are aggressive and competitive, then you could focus on any of the cooling and comforting *Shanti* mantras. Likewise, if you are fearful and insecure, then look for the stimulating and clarifying *Shakti* mantras. (When in doubt, use A-U-M. It's a complete and balanced mantra. No other is considered complete without it!) Basically, you have to see where you are and where you'd like to be. Then use suitable mantra vehicles to cover that distance.

Mantras can eventually help you make up your mind to take positive measures in some sphere of your life. Likewise, music can put you in the mood to make changes where needed.

MUSIC

Whereas the way of mantras is a more conscious approach to taming the mind, the way of music is a more lilting one to liberating it. Mantras elevate your thoughts while music energizes your feelings. Adolescent or adult, we all are drawn toward music likewise. It's a language we all may not fluently speak, but it's one we all understand.

Music can mesmerize the most truant among us. In my neighborhood church, I would often spot a sprightly group of youngsters pour in for the Sunday mass. The only peculiar behavior was that they would come at the same time and leave within half an hour. Intrigued, I investigated, and found that they came in when the choir started to sing and scrammed out when the speeches began!

However, music is very much part of our ordinary speech too. Music therapist and pianist Eric Barnhill says that "musical nuance" in fact facilitates our brains "to process and organize a large and complex variety of material ..."[13] In the absence of such structuring, our comprehension actually drops by 70 percent![14] So if I were to listlessly read an essay, it will be like an undifferentiated heap of sounds that won't make much sense to either you or me. But if I nuance this text with intonations and pauses, which are musical tenets, our understanding will increase.

Musical structures, a la visual structures, also make it easy for you to memorize and recall. Students of yore would memorize entire epics, as they had both "rhythm and rhyme"[15] as says author and neurologist Oliver Sacks. Now we too can recall poems and songs heard in childhood. In fact, even those who have suffered a memory loss can recall songs without forgetting, and those who have stutters can sing smoothly without faltering. Interestingly, there seem to be "more efficient mechanisms in auditory memory than in visual memory."[16] Your brain can remember complex multi-tonal sounds to a far greater degree than you it can even register visual change.[17]

Our emotions and feelings are the musical aspects of our speech. So love-loaded words like "my dear," "sweetie" falls like music on another's ears. To relate with even a stronger sense of connection and weaken ego barriers, employ the musical channel of relational names. In India, that's quite the norm. Instead of generic "aunts" and "uncles," we have special names for different relationships. So an older sister would be called Didi; the mother's sister would be called Ma-si, meaning "like mother," etc. Now these names add a personal touch to your address and equation, reduce ego barriers and facilitate trust. What's more interesting is that you can call any elderly lady your *didi* or sister and any other man your *bhaiya* or brother and it will unleash the same energies of affection. The newly appointed sister or brother will instantly become more concerned and charitable toward you.

Music stimulates your brain and nervous system. Alfred Tomatis, the pioneering figure of modern music therapy, says that singing is "the best way to provide our nervous system with the high-quality stimulation that is indispensable to optimal functioning," even if you sing casually.[18] Singing plays a therapeutic role as well. It de-stresses by blocking "a lot of the neural pathways that pain travels through,"[19] as says music therapist Patricia Preston-Roberts. Once you do start enjoying singing, you can record your feelings before and after the event—what appeared to you grave earlier will feel much lighter now. Singing sharpens your hearing too. You must be able to hear the notes to reproduce them. This aural acuity is also the reason why singers have a developed capacity to pick up new accents. And drop them too!

On another note, the sound of your voice reveals the state of your spirit. According to Suzanne Sterling, a yoga and voice teacher, if you utter more of the deeper pitches, your spirit has more gravitas and could do with more lightheartedness and playfulness. And if you are relying more on the higher pitches, then you need to ways to ground yourself. So just like you correct your nutritional imbalance with multivitamins, you can balance your energies by listening to or expressing sounds that you ordinarily exclude.[20]

However, how you sound is a consequence of how you are feeling within. If you have empathy at your core, you will sound concerned. If you have insecurity at your core, you will sound malicious and mean. Not just in speech, but also even in music, your state of mind is what gives a different flavor to your music. As Hazrat Inayat Khan points out in "The voice of a sympathetic singer is quite different from one who is heartless."[21]

Music balances our time-perspective. Author, psychologist, and professor emeritus at Stanford Phillip Zimbardo tells us that we all divide events unfolding in time consciously or unconsciously into the zones of past, present, and future. Instead of being overly present-oriented, future-oriented, or past-oriented, the more optimal or happiness-inducing way, he suggests, is to have a bit of all three is this proportion: past-positive-oriented (gives roots), with a moderate future-focus (gives wings), and a moderate present-involvement (gives energy).[22] Prof. Zimbardo urges each one of us to realize which time zones are excessive or deficient in our life, and suitably balance. Music training can indeed help you strike the optimal balance.

Listening to music can equally hone your musical competencies. It exposes you to the musical language of harmony and rhythm, and thus makes your grasp of them better. Of course, musical training of any kind will further train your ear for harmony and heighten its intuitive awareness of harmony or lack of it. In fact, even if you start learning to play an instrument now, you will acquire adeptness sooner than you think! Dr. Alvaro Pascual-Leone at Harvard has shown that even people with no prior musical training achieved near-perfect skills in a week with just a few hours of daily practice![23]

However, for sustained benefits, you need you need long-term commitment. But it's worth it for added reasons. Long hours of music practice have also been found to generate more gray matter in different parts of your brain.[24] Music, which involves understanding of proportions and harmonies, further improves your ability to reason and evaluate. A Swedish study found a link between your sense of rhythm and your reasoning and problem-solving skills.[25] So music makes you smarter!

In addition to improving your brain's abilities, music also augments your body's agility. Moving atypically, but naturally in response to different music, coaxes your carriage out of conditioning, encourages you to become more flexible in body and mind, and makes you more confident. All this is invigorating. In study in Switzerland which investigated the effect of the Dalcroze method of movement on geriatrics that they walked out of the class with a gait "as if they're at least twenty years younger."[26]

Dance, aided usually by music, counters decay and stagnation in our body and thus mind. Author Judith Lynne Hanna says, dance symbolizes the victory of "life and health forces over those of disease and death."[27] In one ancient cult, she informs, religious statues are periodically removed from their usual place and made to dance as puppets with a view to "animate them, vitalize them and give them life."[28]

Significantly, music is a great example of a situation where the laws and the limitations end up liberating one most. Indeed, in music, your options are the least: the same notes, a few scales and some rhythms. Yet, explorations here always lead you to someplace new. The creative possibilities of music, despite the limitations (or because of them), are almost inexhaustible.

Likewise, as you become conscious of your boundaries of behavior and conduct and cultivate a commitment to harmony at all times, you too will pass the tests of patience and trials of the ego. In any case, they are obstacles placed on your path to provoke your greater potential. Yet if you get provoked, the creative provocation is lost. That's why you need to cultivate a deep core of inner silence—so that you can hear even noise like music.

MEDITATION

Studies tell us that "continuous melodic flow," whereby there isn't space and time for silence and absorption of the music, actually "allows our attention to wander, and overall cognitive activity is surprisingly subdued during these periods."[29] That is why traditional systems of music incorporate meditative moments as part of the melodic framework.

Importantly, the restless melodic movement can be seen as an allegory for the relentless activity in our lives. Here too, if we do not provide ourselves with enough moments of absorption and assimilation—provided passively through sleep and relaxation and consciously through meditation and creative hobbies— we risk thinking and behaving from inner stress and not creativity.

Meditation is a site of mediation between your spirit and your soul. Opening the sluice gates of your soul will flush you with healing energies, just like opening the windows of your house at dawn floods it with soft light and fresh air. And then you will see things and events the way you see them after a restful sleep—hopefully and cheerfully.

Importantly, meditation nurtures your inner depth. Ordinarily, experiences of loss, lack and limitations mellow us and take us deeper within. Meditation is a positive way to cultivate the same depth. At a physical level, meditation stimulates the production of melatonin, the pineal gland's secretion that restores vitality and counters ageing. However, its production diminishes with the onset of puberty. Meditation and relaxation can trigger it again.

To meditate, ideally, take out time for it, just like you take out time to eat or work. For a general technique, sit comfortably on a chair or on a mat on the floor with your back against the wall. Support yourself with props like cushions or blankets to maintain comfort and uprightness. Distance yourself from distractions: put your phone on silent mode, use eye covers and ear plugs, choose a dimly lit and quiet space, and drop all worries (you can call them back later!). Make the moment feel special. It's your date with your soul—your best friend ever. Light a candle, keep a vase of flowers, play soothing music and simply be at peace in the moment. Enjoy the security and unconditional acceptance of your soul. It's like cosmic maternal womb. Forgive yourself amply.

Free yourself of your fears through accepting them or surrendering to the will of the universe.

Outside the formal practices, you can meditate in freewheeling ways too: under the shower, during the stroll from the subway station to home, or while having a cup of tea. As we say in India, any time that you think of god or thank the forces of the universe is a moment of meditation. Even piecemeal actions count. Their 'calories' even get stored in you and release energy when you need.

Sometimes sounds can be therapeutic in moments when silence feels scary. If you live alone or stay in an isolated part of the town, you may like to switch on the TV or play music upon coming home. To some even the familiar buzz of the air conditioner or fan is comforting. I recall this funny episode in a silent Indian film[30] where the protagonist, a slum dweller, gets himself in a situation where he can pose as a rich man and have access to his luxury and comforts. Yet, habituated to the hustle and bustle of the slums, he can't sleep in the pin-drop silence of his new habitat. So he goes back to the slums, records the noises, and plays that as lullaby to help him sleep! Thus, liberally use sounds that relax you. Relaxation is half way to meditation.

It is useful to meditate upon values that you'd like to imbibe. So you could reinforce in yourself the values of compassion, humility, kindness et al. In the receptive state of meditation, your mindset can be easily reprogrammed. Use role-models to behold these values in action. For instance, you may like this person's cheerful nature. Visualize it a few times and you will find yourself becoming more cheerful and enthusiastic. Likewise, you might like another person's ability to remember birthdays and write thank you notes. Imbibe that too!

Indeed, when you meditate upon a specific thought, like for the welfare of all, then your brain absorbs that message so deeply that it is always in a state of readiness to deliver it. The mantra becomes ingrained. Your greater mindfulness also translates into more presence of mind. Long-term mediators have in fact been found to have greater gamma activity in the brain, leading to holistic and healthy perceptions.

Meditation helps you to develop a rapport your solitude and silence. Ordinarily, we feel the need to constantly talk or be in the company of others. We lose our sense of self if we aren't expressing or exhibiting who we are. Meditation will help foster your friendship with your inner silence. Then, you will not feel threatened by it!

This love for silence—when you look forward to it and actively seek its company—will then counter your hyper-vigilance (which drives the hyper-activity in mind and speech as well). I want to share this simple and clear definition of hyper vigilance provided by Dr. Barry Quinn:

"The definition of hyper vigilance is someone who cannot turn off his or her mental activity for any length of time. They must always be thinking or focusing on something. They tend not to be able to let go of emotional issues but rather obsess relentlessly about them. ... It is very hard for them to relax and unwind. Therefore, they generally have a lot of sleep disorders as well. Anything that would increase their Alpha waves would be very beneficial to them." [31]

It is important to remember that silence, security and inner comfort do not dull your power to think or act. Inner silence can actually make you all the more conscious of the bigger picture, and thus enable your better sense. Indian Guru Sri Sri Ravishankar says, "If you want to make sense, it has to come from silence." [32] When you can remain silent within, you can endure situations or people and handle them without losing your peace. Just action and subtle correction will come naturally and quietly.

So add muscle to your meditation so that you can access your inner silence in a variety of situations, no matter how noisy or negative. Yogi Bhajan says, "Meditation is not what you do in the morning." [33] It is "the daily result of that practice."[34]

I tried this exercise in a challenging situation to improve my access to my inner silence. I scheduled my meditation practice on the night of Diwali, the beginning of the Indian New Year, which is marked by festivities and in our modern living firecrackers as well. So meditation wasn't certainly going to be easy. That was precisely the point!

So I took the help of calming music to connect to buffer the outside noise. Calming and poetic autosuggestions can also work well. Gradually, the din outside (or my inner agitation!) seemed to subside. Correspondingly, I was bothered less by the same situation. The comforting absorption in my inner self prevented me from over-hearing and over-reacting to the outer events. My awareness arrived midway between calmness within and connection without. That's where it needs to stay!

A MUSICAL LIFE

In Indian treatises on music, it is in effect the human body and being that is considered as the foremost musical instrument. Music, mantras, and meditation are important means to tune this instrument. They will enable you to have mindful and musical approaches toward the diversity of life. The latter will then become a fantastic ally in your creative growth.

Finally, just like there are no good or bad tones; there are in effect no good or bad situations or people. How you engage with your given material depends on your sensibility. Just like a knife can be used to hurt or heal, so can any situation be harnessed to block or release. By inviting a musical sensibility, you will avoid so many blocks that you would have otherwise bumped into and breakthrough a lot of traps that you could have otherwise fallen into. Stay with me!

Music is the expression of harmony in sound. Love is the expression of harmony in life.
—Stephen F. Gaskin[35]

CHAPTER 8
AWAKENING YOUR MUSICAL SENSIBILITY

The advantageous role of music in human evolution is evident by the fact that your brain is primed for music. Daniel J. Levitin, author, musician, and cognitive neuroscientist tells us "all of us are expert musical listeners … even when we're unable to articulate the reasons why,"[36] In fact, a variety of pitches are mapped on different areas of our brain.[37] Even two-day-old infants have an ear for music, and show their likes and dislikes![38] It is this inherent musical capacity that helps you to detect a range of frequencies and "recognize hundreds of different voices."[39] That's how you can even hear the undercurrent of emotions in people's voices and know how they are feeling.[40] Now all that remains is honing this innate ability and making use of it in your real life.

The ways of receiving and expressing that I propose will build your motivation for seeking harmony and symphony, supremely musical aims. You will foster the musical habits of inclusion, accommodation, positive play, dialogue and smooth integration. You will learn here how to create it in your daily living through the musical means of acceptance, adjustment and alchemy.

As you act and create with an active and sensitive awareness, you will surely experience that good begets good, respect begets respect, smile begets smile, and giving begets giving. Let's make life this hearty!

HEAR FROM YOUR HEART!

I recall this elderly musician's concert where my colleague was irritated by the breathlessness of the singer and wondered why he insisted on singing at his age, whereas I was appreciative of the fact that the singer could sing with such energy despite his age. Both of us emphasized different things, depending on how we heard. I used my heart while he used his head. In effect, I saw the singer with a considerate eye while my colleague saw him with a critical one.

Now music heals you because it moves your heart and mellows your feelings. The aspect of caring and reaching out is intrinsic to music. That is why music has universal appeal. When you respond to a song, you feel it belongs to you, notwithstanding who wrote it, who composed it or who sang it. You appropriate it, as you own. This quick integration with a healing force heals you almost instantly.

Now your heart is your own healing force. When your ego is creating troubles for you (situations too trouble us because our ego is resisting and not accepting), you need to rush to the solace of your heart. Then you will bypass the head that is judging the situation or people as good or bad. The heart will make you see your situation or others with a wholesome considerate eye and not just a critical regard.

Use this state to receive impressions. The Tomatis effect (named after Dr. Alfred Tomatis, who discovered this relationship) tells us that you can only express and perpetuate those sounds you are capable of hearing in the first place. However there is a challenge: our auditory pathway, unlike the visual one, crosses the brain's hot-center for fear and anxiety, the amygdales that are situated near the ears, and which affect our entire nervous system. To make it more challenging, you brain is geared to catch the discordant note (the evolutionary purpose being to spot threats and disharmony). And when you hear the discordant note, it instantly activates your anxiety center.

To toughen matters further, just like our seeing is colored by our preconceptions and associations, so is our hearing. That means that if you do not have a good image of a certain person, then even when he or she is saying something pertinent or doing good things, you will not receive his or her words or gestures with appreciation. This even holds in case of music, where one might believe that it's the music and not the musician that counts. Hardly so! Studies tell us how much our tastes in music (and other art) are influenced by what we think of the artist. Einstein once expressed thus about a fellow musician (yes, he was a musician too!): "To me his musical personality is indescribably offensive so that for the most part I can listen to him only with disgust."[41]

Evidently, your hearing is rather influenced by your prejudices and associations, much in the way seeing is. You thus need to play an active part in processing what you hear, just as you do for how you see. Because both are affecting how you feel.

Now just like iron cuts iron and images cut images, sounds indeed cut sounds. Positive affirmations, mantras, mind games, music, and the sound of silence can counter the noises of your insecure and easy to rattle ego.

Your inner silence will awaken your tolerance and patience. I remember this incident where this lady in a congregation was behaving very rudely with people around. And I was sitting right next to her! This lady started objecting to any thing and every thing I was doing. But I was doing nothing to hurt her. However, given my sensitivity to vibes, I felt an interpersonal challenge coming way.

Sensing my own inner unrest in this situation and my possible overreaction, I became utterly silent, and steadily went closer to my heart. I used a calming and motivating mantra that said: "It's okay. It's okay. It's your challenge for the day! Pass it with flying colors!" As I became a little more secure, and the flush of my face receded, I used a mind game to imagine that this lady was going through a personal crisis and was therefore upset and unhappy. She was just venting it on me. I also saw her in the image of my own mother. That made me concerned about her negative state of mind. My unrest went away. As a result, I remained kind toward her.

To buttress my positive state, I turned for solace toward this cherubic girl seated just behind me. So this little angel became my goddess of energy. I refueled myself by playing and laughing with her. Other people joined in too. In a while, perhaps due to my lack of negative response or given my budding circle of friends, my angry and unhappy neighbor took a U-turn: from being dominating and disrespectful, she switched to being gracious and genuine. Seeing me not fall for her provocation, she rose above too! She began to make conciliatory gestures toward me. Of course I accepted.

ALERT LISTENING

The other day, this friend of mine called to ask me if I knew a doctor to help cure a cyst. Now just a day before another common friend had been diagnosed with a cyst and had spoken to me about it. Thinking that my friend was referring to this friend of ours, I waxed eloquent on the course of action that this friend had already discussed with me, and blah blah. At the end of it, my friend meekly rejoined: "I know about her cyst. I am calling about mine."

If only we'd listen! But we are in such a hurry to express that we hear just about approximately. So the first thing is to exercise speech-control like the way you do portion control!

Lack of a listening temperament makes us refer to past knowledge and not be in the moment. As Sean Connery in a film, "When we don't understand, we turn to our assumptions."[42] To prevent your assumptions from freezing into dogma and making your spirit inflexible, you need to keep assimilating new information. By developing a listening temperament, you will become alert to it and even consciously seek it.

Both listening and observation are the receptive aspects of hearing and seeing respectively. They foster your sensitive and vigilant awareness of yourself and your world. In fact, listening empowers your visual observation too. It can help you collate information from various frames and improve your understanding of the bigger picture. In the Indian film *Firaaq*,[43] this musician tells his Man Friday, who is captivated by the ready-to-consume news offered by television: "If you learn to listen… you'll know more about the world."[44]

However, in order to listen with justness, we need to distinguish between what is being said, and what we think is being said. Now see this exchange between a customer and a seller at a flea market.

Buyer: *How much is this bangle for?*

Seller: *Ten dollars.*

Buyer (genuinely): *Will it rust?*

Seller (screaming): *What else do you expect in ten dollars!*

Since I was present on this occasion, I heard what may not be ringing as loud here. The seller's infuriated reply came in the wake of what he heard in his head, and not necessarily to what was actually said. His annoyed response was a result of his own exaggerated reaction to the poor buyer's innocent question. He 'heard' him as insinuating that his wares weren't of good quality. And this imagined pre-judgment prejudiced his hearing. His overreaction ended up creating bad vibes between him and his customer, and the latter walked away. Both lost out on what could have been an energizing experience of give and take.

This kind of listening is not peculiar to the market but is typical of most of our interactions. Instead of listening to others with openness, we listen to them in the company of our whispering fears and insecurities.

The way out is to listen what is being said. If you think there is an element of the "unsaid", or you feel that the other is trying to say something in between the lines, then by all means seek clarification. But do so in a guileless and straightforward spirit: the way children do. This manner can disarm one and all. At other times, even if you can hear the unsaid, keep it to yourself! As a thumb rule, listen more and react less.

To encourage listening with innocence, cultivate inner quiet. *Pranayama* or breath-regulating exercises will help you to slow down your exhalations and thereby your urge to over express. There is also a fast from speech that requires you to observe silence for a sustained period, be it a day, half-a-day, or just a couple of hours. It deepens your rapport with your inner self and inner voice.

Retention of the breath is in effect an advanced yoga technique[45] to develop strength of mind. Swami Sivananda gives the illuminating example of a "porter carrying heavy bags of rice or wheat at the wharf (who) instinctively fills his lungs with air and practices unconscious retention of breath."[46] Indeed, you spontaneously go inward and unconsciously hold your breath whenever you are preparing to give your best—going to the stage before a performance, entering the boss's room to ask for a raise, or diving into the pool for the first time. So your restraint is strengthening.

Now a listening temperament doesn't mean that you won't be participative. On the contrary, you are going to be hyper-present—

your entire being turned into an attentive medium of reception. With a keen listening, you will sense, see and learn much more about your environment. This greater knowledge will enhance your ability to influence. And you thought the one who speaks has power!

To perk up your listening, you can also replace some of your time spent watching news on television by hearing the news on radio. (Tough one!) Studies tell that listening to audio "demands a heightened form of concentration," and thus better absorption.[47] Or you can read stories to your children. Reading will fire your imagination. A study says that you indeed "see" and "hear" the story or the situation as you are reading it.[48]

You can also depend more on your hearing in daily routines. So deliberately shut your eyes in short tasks like combing your hair or putting cream on your hands and face. Feel your skin or the sensations on your scalp. Become attentive to yourself in a deeper way.

Maintain a calm ambience at home or at work. The street is noisy enough. (Unless you live on a lonely one!) Studies show that it is our continued over-exposure to loud sounds that eventually dulls our hearing as we age. Now if you work in a factory or on a shop floor, where you can't help the noise, create a little room that serves as your cocoon of silence. If you are unable to do that, soak for twenty minutes in relaxed silence upon reaching home.

Invest in a musical instrument. Play on it or sing with it. Musical training makes your listening even sharper. You will be able to hear and pick musical strains over and above the general commotion. As the musical prodigy in the film *August Rush* (2007) says, "Listen. Can you hear it? The music. I can hear it everywhere. ... It's all around us. All you have to do is open yourself up. All you have to do ... is listen."[49]

Learning new languages works just as well for mental acuity and flexibility. Studies also tell us how multilingual children have better cognitive skills, memory, and communication and listening skills.[50] A girl once told me that she found Indians to be much more intuitively linked to others. I do think that their greater exposure to different languages does make their hearing keener, which in turn enables their quicker adaptation and integration with their environment. Now an infant in India is exposed to at least two or three languages from birth. To add to the tonal complexity, even the same language, in the same household, is likely to be spoken with different accents, intonations, and emphases, given the intermingling of regional influences. Then even as adults, many among us cross-regions in search of education or work, and so need to quickly learn new languages. In fact, Indians who are otherwise illiterate can fluently converse in about five to six languages! I once asked one barely educated cab driver about how much time he took to learn a new language. And he said, "Long. About six months." Gosh!

Finally, encourage a listening culture in a group by paying respectful attention to others and allowing every one their say in the matter. Reduce your love for listening to your own voice. Spend time with your inner voice.

Also, listen with awareness of the underlying dynamics. If you are listening to your competitor's thoughts on you, don't expect generosity! And if you are listening to an admirer's words, don't take them too seriously! Avoid listening to excessive criticism of others. Dwelling on what is bad in others is a least effort approach. The greater effort consists in building upon the slightest strand of opportunity. So change the goal post if conversations are going awry or becoming negative.

And when you need to express—which you must—use the following guidelines for simple, effective and vital exchange.

AUTHENTIC AND TRANSPARENT COMMUNICATION

Some years ago I was with a group of kindergartners. It was my first time ever with such a group. Now these thunderous kids were making a lot of ruckus, and I wanted them to become quiet so that I could talk to them. But all my strategies were insufficient. Exhausted and miffed, I said in my sarcastic best: "So I guess you all want me to go from here." And this time they all heard me! In chorus, they sang, "Bye, bye, ma'am."

I asked for it! Children can't hear sarcasm or double entendres. That is why they took my offer at face value!

Unclear tones and mixed up agendas in speech confuse the listener. He or she then does not know what to make of what you mean. Such speech is considered a major cause of schizophrenic tendencies.

So foster a culture of clear exchange in your family and among colleagues. Positive and sincere speech is akin to music in its effect—it relaxes false pretensions and encourages people to be authentic. So if you are late for work, give a sincere reason. When you tell the truth, others usually buy it.

But what about times when you are in a bad mood? Should you be clear about that as well? Well, instead of putting on an air of being positive, express your ill ease. Studies tell us that if you set up an inner dichotomy—feeling and thinking negatively, but pretending to be positive—then you will strengthen your negative thinking all the more![51] So come up with your problems for sure. But just so that you can come out of them!

As far as possible, say what you mean. When you say one thing and mean quite another—as in sarcastic speech—you're actually setting up rhythms of neurosis and mistrust in society. You're adding confusion to the chaos and distorting your own playing field. Sending mixed signals will mess up your own mind as well; mixing up your main goals with your marginal ones. So don't feel compelled to add that jumble of extra vibes. In wanting to say too much, you might end up saying nothing at all!

Above all, bring credibility to your words. So when you say, "I'll call you tomorrow," do call up the next day. And even if it slips your mind, promptly apologize for the slip. In fact, when you admit your mistake, others will come to your rescue to make you feel better about it. But if you try to gloss over your mistake, others will look through it, and might see you with prejudice as a result.

Just like you need to say sorry with feeling, express your thanks with feeling too. In any case, people feel and receive your energy much more than they receive your words. Also, when you feel the thankfulness from deep within, you etch it in your awareness—you feel it for longer.

Also, being a positive person does not mean that you have to say yes to everything. Say no if that's what you want to say. But you can always say it in a way that sounds nice! Even so, your 'no' might hurt someone in that moment. But if you frankly explain yourself, gently assert yourself, or playfully express yourself, then others will come to respect your stance and value your frankness. I remember from many years ago an uncle who would always give a candid response when my mother would tell him "so nice of you to call upon us," and he would say in a jovial way, "I called because I needed your help!" We always had a good laugh, never for a moment holding his forthrightness against him.

Even when you need to breakaway from a relationship, give honest reasons for doing so, instead of hiding behind false excuses or finding scapegoats. The other person will even empathize with you, or at least hold least ill will against you. If you feel that someone is giving false excuses, interrogate him or her with patience and openness. Don't be in a hurry to accuse!

Then, whenever you want to speak about an experience that you've had, speak with the intent to enlighten and explain, not to show off or make others feel inferior. And if others are feeling bad for having missed out on the experience that you've had, describe and share it generously with them so that they can feel a part of it. As a thumb rule, include and not alienate.

Nonetheless, there will be still be moments of misunderstanding. You cannot help such situations but you can prevent them through open and clear communication. A lot of understanding can be unleashed when we simply express our preferences and give our reasons for doing or avoiding something. Take this example. You all are going out for a film, and you've arrived at the film-theater in just a nick of time. You still need to park your car, though. In the space that you spot, you need to be mindful of leaving space for easy exiting of all members in the car. You may also be thinking about causing the least inconvenience to the person who may need to reverse his car that's parked next to yours. Besides, you need to leave more room on the left side of the car so that you give your arthritic mother more space to exit. But despite all your sensitive thinking, you may still have your kids in the backseat glowering "Dad! What are you up to? We'll get so late for the film if you never end up parking!"

Instead of getting hurt in this situation, or answering back in annoyed tones, brace up and explain yourself. The fact that you have the film tickets in your pocket will hold your audience captive! To explain yourself better, you can also play a game to bring on a moment of realization—park your car in a way that you jam their exit. They'll will now realize the value of your actions and become tolerant toward the delay thus caused.

Moreover, we all have different likes and dislikes. Even good friends who otherwise have a lot in common may have different preferences. One may pester you to know the story of a movie that you saw, while the other may fight with you for posting the plot on your blog! So please tell/ask others what you/they like. How else will we all know!

And yes, you can be expressive, without being aggressive. You can defend, without being defensive. You can oppose, without being oppressive.

At any moment that you feel anger surging (it happens!), simply lower your voice, become silent, deliberately insert caring and playful tones, and feel that you are with family. You'll cool down!

Just remember that your speech has a warm and easily excitable nature. That's what gives your speech its creative power. The act of speech is creating new realities. It is bringing out your inner thoughts and making them evident even to you. So enable this creative process by keeping rudeness, pettiness, hurtful barbs and aggressive tones out of the way. Whenever they arise, stop talking. Or change the topic!

Also remind yourself that in a heated frame of mind, you might say things to others that will either boomerang or leave you regretful later. I read of someone who was couldn't overcome his deep guilt for having asked a friend to "get lost." For that evening, his friend was lost forever.

There is a thin line even between passion and aggression. Stay aware of it. I once met a green activist who was so incensed over the lack of eco-friendliness in our lives that he could hardly inspire positive action with his message. People shied away from asking questions and were in dread of him. So while it is good to work for peace, it is far better to work with it!

You might suspect that all this behavior will make you a misfit. On the contrary! In fact, your refreshing example will encourage others to drop their pretensions and get real. So take the lead in setting a climate of naturalness. You'll find others more than willing to support it.

Next is this great way to positively transform—or creatively re-interpret—all kinds of negative feelings. The way poets, and even lawyers, do!

LYRICAL LIES!

This one is my favorite. It is about training your mind to see "something good in everything." By using whatever works!

In India, if a bird dropping falls on your crisp white shirt or freshly washed hair, an onlooker will reduce your despair by saying: "That's a sign of good luck!" Or if you've lost your wallet in a busy marketplace, people will try to cheer you up by saying that you must in fact owe that money to someone from a previous lifetime, and so it's actually quite good that you have now repaid your debt. From feeling upset, you begin to feel relieved!

Lyrical lies are basically creative interpretations or inventions of thought that are aimed at talking yourself (and others) out of your state of discomfort, stress and thus suffering. Eventually, just like visualization improves your perceptions, lyricization uplifts your vibrations. Both strengthen your mind and spirit.

Now it doesn't matter whether your lyrical suggestion is 'true' or not. It's more important that your mantra or thought liberates you from fear and helps you handle the situation to the best of your ability—from your truer core.

To interpret problems positively, you just need your good intentions in place. When you have a sincere wish to cheer up yourself or others, you are bound to find a way. A little girl once began crying when a famous person, guest at an event, did not give her an autograph. I held her in my arms and told her that because she was tiny and standing among other tall people, the star did not even get a chance to see her. And so he didn't ignore her, as she felt, but simply didn't see her in the crowd. The girl was comforted. She smiled, energizing me in return.

Another example concerns a young girl who once dreamt that she'd become blind. When she narrated the dream fearfully to her mother, the latter was smart enough not to fan her fears. Instead, she gave the whole thing a spin. She wondered aloud if such a dream could mean that her daughter's third eye of intuition was about to open. The mother's positive interpretation cast a doubt in the girl's negative outlook. Her despair gave way to excitement. In fact, she asked her mother if the third eye will allow her to foresee the questions appearing in her exam!

A similar example is from one Hindi film[52] where a young boy confronting a ghost refuses to believe that he's seeing a ghost. The boy insists that there are only angels and no ghosts, as his mother has told him so. This young boy's positive thinking is so contagious that the ghost starts doubting his identity and begins to behave like an angel!

So next time when your friends express some doubts, realize that your response will determine the direction their mind takes. Your words and thoughts are like mantras then! You may have seen that when you cheer up your friend with words like, "I believe in you," or, "You are a gem of a person," then your words can make a world of a difference to another's.

Sometimes your lovely lies are preferable to the troubling truth. I remember an instance where an uncle of mine was recovering from a serious heart attack and was still hospitalized. Relatives were deliberating two courses of action—faithfully tell him the fact of his condition, or not. Now the impact of hard-hitting facts can be softened through feelings. And these feelings can help the other to receive the factual truth in a positive spirit. So in my brief meeting with him, I said: "Your heart just got younger by ten years after your operation!" On his face, still shadowed by the anesthesia, a faint smile broke. I saw in that moment his heart beating for life again.

The poetic salve can soothe and give hope. I use it in cases where I see people feeling bitter or thinking negatively. For example, when I hear people blaming their parents or siblings for all that has gone wrong with their lives, I share with them this Indian thought, which says that it is in effect your own soul that chooses where it will be born and what kind of challenges it will face. The soul knows what kind of experiences will help it to help evolve. People usually have a breakthrough moment with insight. As they assume more responsibility for their given situation, they aren't frustrated or bitter anymore. They contemplate positive responses, which sparks off growth and renewal in many spheres. Thus, lyrical lies, aimed at uplifting false and negative attitudes, can enable us in profound and prophetic ways.

Liberally use lyrical thoughts to liberate yourself of animosity, fear, ill-will or anger. Not only will you avoid negative thoughts, you will also use their stimuli for building your creative muscle. For example, in the blockbuster Hindi film, *Three Idiots* (2009), the protagonist repeats the mantra, "All is well!" to keep panic at bay at all times. So you too can develop a handy repertoire of refrains that you can repeat to yourself in situations where you are feeling let down, hurt, betrayed, or left out ... Some lines can be: "The universe loves me even if s/he doesn't!"; "If I am still living with my negative impulses despite my best efforts to improve, why expect others to become better in the snap of a finger!"; "Well, if she is getting compliments and I am not, then she must be deserving it in some way and for some reason!"; "Let me do more good deeds to get the universe to rain goodies on me!"; "I am going to make this work, no matter what."

An elderly lady once told me that whenever she feels hurt about someone betraying or bad-mouthing her, she tells herself this: "When people slander me, they are actually swiping away my karmic debts. Their negative action cancels my negatives. They are doing me a favor! So I need to be grateful to them and certainly not hold grudges." In doing so, she refuses to be pulled down by negativity, be it from others or herself. Little wonder that she looks like an energetic 30 years old despite being 50!

Likewise, another lady once told me that she is pretty happy to have a headache or cold, and doesn't stay in bed feeling depressed. In fact, she makes herself believe that she is actually getting rid of toxins through these micro problems, which otherwise might accumulate and manifest in macro ways. She appears to be almost looking forward to her next headache!

Make up wild reasons to discourage your negative thinking. So you too can make yourself believe that for every negative feeling you harbor, you are inviting a strand of gray hair and a facial wrinkle. You'll drop your worries like a hot potato! Or if your spouse's snoring is bothering you every night, make your peace with it by throwing a lyrical light on it. Tell yourself that it is a healing sound that is magically detoxifying your body. You'll certainly become more sympathetic toward the snoring. Basically, when you can't help it, make it good enough to gulp it.

A question: how is seeing with "colored glasses" any different from poetic inventions? Both are similar in their effect, but in the first case, you play unconsciously into the hands of your prejudices and impulses, while in the second you play consciously with your positive thoughts. Colored glassed weaken your thinking while lyrical inventions energize it.

However, in your bid to overlook the negative, don't stop looking! Take this instance: I was in a stationery store once looking for a brightly covered notebook. Committed to a seeing positively in my mind, I ignored the realities on ground. So the moment I spotted a notebook with a yellow cover and some design, I sighed with satisfaction: "Ah! That's a happy cover." "Not for this one," said a gentle voice from behind. A lady who'd been watching me pointed out with great ease what I had completely missed seeing: a blob of blood-red color, meandering all over the cover—which signified the blood of a dying deer who'd just been struck by a hunter, also shown in the picture. I overlooked something so obvious because I was looking out excessively for what I wanted to see.

That's why you need to smarten up your head even as you sweeten your heart.

SMART LISTENING

Connie Tomaino, director of the Institute for Music and Neurologic Function in New York City, considers music as "brain aerobics," as playing any piece of music requires a musician to process multiple sensory inputs.[53] Studies tell us that working in sync with rhythms "involves brain areas associated with anticipation, attention, movement, timing and ordinal mapping."[54] Indian Maestro for Dhrupad, a meditative style of music, Zahiruddin Dagar is said to have once remarked that "tuning the tanpura (or any other instrument) creates intelligence."[55] This kind of parallel processing, acute listening, and coordinated performance can boost your capacity of integrating diverse inputs in a smooth and judicious blend.

As pianist and conductor Daniel Barenboim says, "Conflict, difference of opinion, is the very essence of music, in the balance, in the dynamic, in the way that the music is written ... Music teaches us that it is precisely our capacity to bring all the different elements together in a sense of proportion so that they lead to a sense of a whole..." [56]

Indeed, Dr. Alvaro Pascual-Leone, professor of Neurology confirms. He tells us that your brain alters fundamentally in response to musical training. In the bargain, it is equipped with a superior "translation mechanism"[57] that can smoothly integrate diverse inputs of information and lead to holistic thinking and action.

Now the fluency and agility with which a musician plays an instrument is seen as comparable to the ease with which you play with language, even in impromptu settings. It's just that music is a more complex language. Like any other language, this one too can be learnt. And because it requires much greater coordination and integration of tone and time, it can build the capacity of your brain to assimilate and integrate, without causing stress or ruffling your peace.

Musical involvement indeed builds your capacity for "thinking concurrently about complex patterns and sensing multiple levels of interaction—holistic thinking—rather than linear, reductionist analysis,"[58] as says Dr. Robert S. Root-Bernstein of Michigan State University while explaining how music making develops divergent or out-of-the-box thinking.[59] Einstein (who played the violin and piano) credited his discovery of relativity to his musical perception.

Intimacy with music also improves your emotional sensitivity. Now musicians can hear the pitches of their strings or keys in ways that we can't. A transfer effect of this intelligence is that they can intuitively sense the layers of emotions embedded in a certain utterance or emotion.[60] So if you say, "I am quite okay, really," a musician will be able to hear the lurking vibrations of sadness or disquiet despite your brave pretense of sounding okay.

Musical exposure and exercise thus enhance your capacity for both thinking and feeling. It thus hones your intuition, or that magic fusion of the intelligence of your head and heart. It sharpens your sixth sense. You will become acutely aware of when things 'sound right' and when they do not.

Musical practice also demands your integrity. Sarod maestro Amjad Ali Khan says, "You can lie through language, but there can be no untruth in music making."[61] In music, you privilege clear and neat sequences and conscious blends and mixtures. It demands that you steer clear of conning and confusing yourself or others. As you become true to yourself, you earn trust from others rather quickly. Your collaborative or symphonic voice thus strengthens, and heightens your creative voice.

As a final word, just months before my grandfather died, he said this in response to my grandmother's query as to why he rehearsed music every day despite his eight decades of experience. He said, "My practice keeps me warmed up to the music inside me and outside me. It helps me sense the path ahead. I need this sense when I move to the world beyond." He left us soon enough, well-equipped to find his way.

MUSIC IN ACTION

Music is also an apt metaphor for the great potential of beauty in our lives that we can create just with our positive intentions, open attitudes and constructive regards. The only challenge is to maintain them in the face of situations that challenge our balance and reduce our positive steam. Yet a fall into negative feelings is also a vital creative motor. For nothing energizes you more than your own rising above.

I offer a tool-kit comprising seven means to make the most of your daily challenges.

At the center of your being, you have unimagined resources.
—Lao Tzu

CHAPTER 9

CREATIVE VIGOR:
ENERGIZE YOUR INFLUENCE

To sustain your creative vision and voice, I summarize here the 'A to G' of a harmonious sensibility. As you tap into any of these seven key attitudes, you will reconnect, in one way or the other, to the music within you, around you and beyond you. It will keep you uplifted.

THE A TO G OF CREATIVE VIGOR

A—Acceptance

B—Better Nature and Better Sense

C—Creation and Collaboration

D—Dreaming and Doing

E—Emptiness and Enthusiasm

F—Faith

G—Gratitude and Giving

A—ACCEPTANCE

Author Larry Dossey narrates a moving story of a famous violinist[62] whose violin strings snapped during a concert. Just when the audience thought it was the end of the show, this violinist, also physically challenged, began to play from his broken violin with "such passion and such power and such purity"[63] that it left the audience in raptures. When he finished he said, "You know, sometimes it is the artist's task to find out how much music you can still make with what you have left."[64]

But for this consciousness of alchemy to arise, acceptance is the first step. It is only because this musician didn't get annoyed or perturbed did he have the inner resources to invent what he did.

When you fully accept a situation for what it is, then its pressure becomes a propelling force, and not a strain. It makes your concentration all the more acute and you can cut through obstacles with your motivation. The push of a challenge is readying you for a quantum leap. You will surely materialize your positive intention, and at times even more.

Yet left to yourself, you wouldn't take such a plunge! I mean you wouldn't willingly break your violin or puncture your car or lose your keys just to challenge yourself. Indeed, no one wants to jump in risky waters. Until they are pushed!

Here is a lighthearted take on it. A man passing by a lake saw a crowd shouting, "Save the boy! He's drowning!" He hastens to get a close look. And lo and behold, we see him jump into the waters. "Brave man!" the crowd squeals. After a ten-minute struggle, the man succeeds in saving the boy and they both come out. This brave man is greeted with cheers and applause. He looks exhausted and waves to signal silence. Still panting, he speaks: "Thanks for the cheers, but who the hell pushed me down there!"

I see the pressures in our life as deliberate pushes and pokes from the cosmos, the ultimate coach. Your inner and outer troubles indeed come to upset your balance. But just so that you can improve on it! Now if someone or something threatens to topple you from your position of balance in a posture of physical exercise, won't you stand more solidly to resist? In doing so, won't you find your greater core strength? You need to do the same when you feel inner unrest in any situation. Instead of denying your feelings or panicking in their wake, recognize them as negative feelings and accept them. Remain mindful that this situation can trigger your growth, if you can rise above. But first you need to lie low.

Here's another interesting take on it. In Indian astrology, *Shani* or Saturn is the planet that is said to give great troubles and cause upheavals (to streamline and discipline us). That's why people fear the transit of Saturn in their life. Yet the best antidote to Saturn's challenges is not fear but acceptance. Then it works for you and not against you. This approach is evident in the way people carry themselves in a *Shani* temple. They hold their hands back and bow their heads, never looking at the deity in the eye. *Shani* is said to burn the one who stares at it: an allegorical way to say that if you fight an aggravated situation in aggressive ways, its destructive potential will increase all the more.

Indeed, in our life too, when moments of annoyance, anger, and agitation arise, they will to more tumult if you respond to them with even more annoyance, anger, and agitation. Instead, bow to them! Refuse to fan the fires. Curtail their perpetuation. Interestingly, in yoga, bowing your head is a *bandha* or energy sealing-in posture; it locks in the coolness of the head and prevents the dissipation of vital heat in the gut. So your head in effect cools down when you bow to a problem and your creative energy is not wasted.

Coincidentally, there is just a 't' separating *Shani* (troubles) and *Shanti* (tranquility). And this 't' is for tolerance! So stir it in when you smell trouble. It will help you to stand still till your inner storm subsides. With your rising inner peace and security, you will take steps to dissipate the outer one. Now it will be its turn to bow out.

Sometimes it is hard to accept negative situations that hit us for no apparent fault of ours, like an earthquake or a freak accident. But you need to understand that your lack of acceptance will only increase your suffering. Help yourself to accept the situation, and even find some good in it. Use mind games and lyrical lies.

Accepting a situation does not mean that you are avoiding or escaping it. You are simply enduring it. Interestingly, the Hindi word for resilience is "sahan-shakti," or the power to bear. What is important to note here is that your forbearance is seen as a *shakti* or a powerful force. Indeed, as you forbear more in daily situation, you will empower your balance. You won't lose it easily then!

Moreover, even though acceptance begins as a strategic tactic to turn away from stress, it gradually turns you toward your soul, this abode of peace and love. That's when your acceptance will give way to compassion. Compassion can make your forgive your worst foes and rise above your worst fears. An ancient Indian aphorism suggests that where there is anger, there is sin, but where there's forgiveness there's 'Him.'

Forgiveness will energize your creative momentum. Just like the processing speed of your computer increases when you delete old files, so too is your creative force enhanced when you erase weighty thoughts from your mind. So reduce the time you take to forgive. Arrive at instant forgiveness!

Also, it's not important that people you've forgiven should appreciate your generosity or should realize their mistake. In your forgiveness is your freedom. To motivate yourself to forgive others in your heart, believe that every time you forgive someone, the universe forgives you as well. It's a deal!

When you forgive others, you give them as well a chance to start afresh. Recall how you felt when someone forgave you. Create that moment of grace for others too.

Finally, your acceptance, tolerance, forgiveness and compassion will remind you that you do not have to win every battle. But then you don't have to lose them all! Accepting does not mean not acting. It is not at odds with engaging. In fact, it is designed to improve your engagement. Now your responses and actions will emerge from your deeper core and you address inclusive aims.

B—BETTER NATURE AND BETTER SENSE

You'll soon realize like I have that anger, aggressiveness, jealousy, pettiness, envy, cowardice, or self-pity, no matter how justified, disengage you from the harmonious whole of nature.

However, there will be times when you do lose your better nature, as in you become annoyed or impatient. Now it's actually a good situation if you can accept your limitations with love and use the inner unrest or feeling of guilt to fan your positive response or resolve. Then your two steps backward would become your stepping-stone to you even better nature. That's the only way to improve your better nature!

But isn't there a dichotomy between what your better nature demands and your better sense deems? For example, your better nature could be urging you to help someone, but your better sense is telling you to that by not helping you will help him or her better? Then what should you do? Do both! Act by your better sense and along with your better nature. Both will end up doing a better job!

I have found a useful formula to engage both. I use a 70 - 30 proportion for my better nature—better sense needs. This means that in any interaction, I remain conscious of the factual details but ever more connected to the compassion of my soul. I advise putting your greater foot in the soul because it will save you from putting it in the mouth!

Eventually, even if you cannot steer a relationship along the positive course with your loving strategies, in upholding your better nature, you will at least avoid the temptation of hurting others. In fact, in most cases, your better nature will end up making a silent appeal to another's. They too will rise above in response to your rising above.

To increase your commitment to your better nature, buttress your reserves of positive energy whenever you can. Take (or fake!) every opportunity to be playful, poetic, productive, humble, helpful, cheerful et al. A well-exercised heart can counter the ego better.

Of course, use you better sense to inform your better nature. Now if your love is spoiling a child, it is not enabling him or her. Likewise, if your better nature is encouraging others to exploit you or take you as a doormat or become irresponsible themselves, then rethink your stance. Perhaps strategic distancing or straight talk or a strategic show of displeasure (but always used like an emoticon, with playfulness, and with forgiveness and compassion in your heart) can trigger conscientious and responsible behavior in the other. Once your better sense has paid off, no need to stay with its constricting stances. Switch wholeheartedly to your expansive better nature. In effect, you'll need to always keep going back and forth between the voice of your head and the voice of your heart. But when in doubt, err on the side of the latter.

At moments when you feel like a misfit or are tired of being positive in a largely negative milieu, repeat this story to yourself to boost your morale. The story goes like this: A saint is meditating with his students by a lake, when a scorpion stings his hand. The saint moans in pain but gently puts the scorpion back in the lake. Again, the scorpion repeats his act. The saint too repeats his and puts it back again in the water. The disciples who are watching this happen over and over again get very agitated. They demand to know why the saint is not hitting back at the scorpion. The saint says: "The scorpion is doing what is in its nature, and I am doing what is in mine."

However, the big difference between the saint and us is this: the saint has succeeded in discovering his better nature while most of us are still not clear about who we are. Many of us are quite vocal about what we do not like, but can we be as vocal about what we stand for and what we truly value and seek to strengthen?

Now the daily dose of negativity we all inhale is more due to the misdirected energies in all us good people. The negativity finds room in our lives because we aren't consumed enough by our positive visions and aren't clear about our own voice. That is why it is so important to find your positive purpose and creative vocations in life. Via them, you will find your truer self.

Remind yourself that once can live up to your better standards, society will have to haul itself up to meet them. Someone once told me that the call center industry had really 'spoilt' the employee culture because of his or her generous perks. And so employees in other sectors had also begun to demand the better offerings and other sectors of the industry were forced to comply. Exactly that will happen when you enforce your better standards. You will spoil your audience. When they see you doing it, they'll have to follow and in turn make others follow.

To further spread and support this positive contagion, cultivate networks with like-minded people. The cumulative energy will create an upward thrust. You'll stay up and about!

C—CREATION AND COLLABORATION

Ever noticed how you feel in a place where there is too much negative energy? You'll feel pulled down no matter how positive you are. Ever noticed how you feel in a place where there is lots of positive energy? You'll feel propelled up no matter how negative you are!

In the company of enthused and positive people, inspired thinking and behavior won't feel an uphill task. In fact, you will now need to outdo other better natures!

A major challenge for creativity is to keep it open to influences. For as you start creating with your unique vision and voice, the resulting conviction in you and increasing admiration from others can give you the illusion of superiority, a kind of 'I-know-it-all." As you resist reinventing yourself, you will gradually stagnate. And you'll also be saddled with an intolerant ego.

So whenever you feel like snubbing someone, or not listen to others, or shut your mind off to another's creative approach, think about this: Does it really matter if you prefer pink and another likes blue? Or does it really matter if you like skiing but another likes trekking? Why can't we revel in the fact that we are all-different and see the world from different lenses!

Let's instead enable the other to find his or her unique direction. Allow the new colors and flavors to emerge. Life will only look and taste better.

Of course, you can always find some limitation or the other with another's approach. But you can find fault with nature too. So you can say that a mango is just like a mango and can't ever be an orange. It wasn't meant to be!

Basically, the difference between positive and negative people is this: the latter are clear about their (narrow) aims and hell-bent on getting there, notwithstanding who they collaborate with. So even though their ideas are egoistic, their execution is not. Let's learn from them!

D—DREAMING AND DOING

Dreams start a new cycle of creation. They bring in the attendant energies of hope and anticipation. They fill in the emptiness. With dreams in your mind, you become once again youthful in heart.

Dreams connect you to the irrational. They warm you up to your risk-taking ability. In your daily rhythms of practicality, you can get overly rational. That is why you need the poetry of dreams—to free your greater vision and foster your passion. Passion is what makes us all work with dedication and daring.

If you can't find a source of passion, then ignite it through dedication—do whatever work you do for someone or something. You will find the passion. There is this touching story doing the rounds of e-mail forwards where this young boy who was not a bright music student at all ended up playing the piano like a prodigy, all because he dedicated his practice and performance to his mother he'd just lost to cancer.

With passion or dedication, dreams will hardly seem impossible or routine will hardly feel like drudgery. Your whole-hearted participation will feel so satisfying that you won't worry over the results or rewards. That's the essence of Indian thought as well—that you needn't worry about getting rewards for your good intentions and actions. Whether you want them or not, they will come!

E—EMPTINESS AND ENTHUSIASM

To create afresh, the old must give way to the new. You too need to empty yourself and fill yourself anew.

So wipe clean the slate of your achievements, and rid yourself of gathered pride. Become open and child-like again. Do not think too much of what you did or created in the past, because that satisfaction can make you smug, blocking your growth.

Emptiness will also make you alert to your environment. Since now you will be more on the lookout for filling it up. And so you will begin to take notice of many things and phenomena that you ignored or took for granted earlier. This sharper sensing will make you receive more from your environment. And grow yet again in response to this new kind of absorption.

Emptying yourself does not mean that you lose all that you've learnt so far. You can't! It's all within you. You are not emptying yourself of your experience. You are simply staying conscious of not becoming complacent, arrogant or fearful.

In fact, in many ancient cultures, including Indian, creativity is seen as an eternal and infinite cosmic force that any one can tap into. When you are receptive, in other words empty of ego and expectations, these forces can pass through you and uplift you.

Instead of gloating over your handful of talents, challenge yourself continuously. Deliberately keep the company of people who have achieved far more than you have and yet show no signs of complacency and arrogance. Be actively interested in what others are doing, instead wanting all the attention for yourself.

However, it can be hard to deal with the emptiness that comes in the wake of situations like a breakup or losing someone. But in effect, in such moments, you can radically redo your life because the force of your feelings is very strong. That's why they say that if pain doesn't kill you, it leaves you stronger. This depth of feeling can make you work harder and emerge wiser, provided you accept your lows and channel them into constructive activities. Just like your car can cover a lot more ground on a day when the roads are vacant, so can you explore new routes and cover more ground when your life looks empty. So fill up your emptiness through work and creation. It will soon turn to enthusiasm.

Eventually, emptiness is a way to become a child again—innocent, alert, keen. So fill up your emptiness through work and creation. It will soon turn to enthusiasm.

To maintain your morale in your lows of emptiness and to ensure that enthusiasm follows, you need an insurance cover—called faith.

F—FAITH

Faith and trust are the prime movers of creativity in every day life. Can you travel in a bus without having faith in the driver? Can you accept a glass of water from your host without trust? Life tenuously moves on these invisible wheels of faith and trust. Try not breaking them.

Foster faith in the forces of existence. You will find it much easier to accept the twists and turns of fate. You feel secure and protected at all times. You will not become easily embittered or lose hope. You will have an easy and friendly rapport with the universe. You'll be able to ask it for help and receive it as well.

But do remember to ask for what you need! There is this Indian story about a queen who complained to god that he came really late while she needed his help much earlier. And god said, "Sweetie, I came when you called for me. It's you who called so late!"

When asking for help, ask with an open mind. Normally we are happy when we get what we want but doubt our faith when we don't. But the whole point of faith is to have some unshakeable and unchangeable anchor. This is what will keep you rooted through the highs and lows of life. So be happy if you receive what you ask for and be okay if you don't. And as they say, if god gave you everything that you asked for, you'd be in a lot of trouble!

To endear yourself to the universe and attract its grace, stay connected on to it through a mindset of gratitude and giving.

G—GRATITUDE AND GIVING

One day, when I returned home looking exhausted, my lady help asked me if something was wrong. I told her that I was stressed about something. In her ardent desire to help me, she gave me her mind. She said: "You are young. You have a house. You eat good food. You have money. You do good work. You have parents. You can eat at a restaurant. You have a car to take you where you like and when you like. Many people I know do not live like that. So please cheer up."

She did for a blessings-recall, just like nutritionists ask you to do a diet recall. Now I felt so full within that instead of being hungry for help, I was aching be of help! Gratitude is about repeating and reinforcing in your imagination all that you have received and continue to receive from nature, people and life; much in the way you thank the lord before a meal.

Giving follows gratitude. I know a lot of people who go to temples to only "give their thanks." Since their sense of gratitude is so acute, they can't seem to ask for anything more. It's what you sometimes feel for people in a foreign land who cared for you like family despite not being so. But when we receive the same kind of love from our parents and friends back home, we take it all for granted! There's a Hindi song that advises us to "consider every bit of time spent on us by another as a favor." Try to imbibe!

In Vedanta, giving back to humanity is not seen as an 'option.' Rather, it is considered as your prime duty toward sustainable co-existence. It makes sense too. How do you keep expecting fruits from a tree without looking after it? To keep receiving love from nature, you have to keep giving love to it as well. It doesn't matter what you give, as long as you have a true and loving desire to give.

In fact, when you have a pure desire to share and distribute, the universe will be happy to route its own offerings to the world through you. At such times, just doesn't make the mistake of seeing yourself as the giver. And if others see you as such, beg them not too! A Bhakti poet once said that when he gives, his gaze is turned toward the ground, lest people see him as the actual giver and not as the medium that he is. Strangely, the more you become a selfless medium; the more the universe will use you as a distribution channel!

It is useful to see the universe as madam chairman and yourself as its dutiful employer. So now your job profile is to work toward her vision of motherhood and love. Find a mission that suits it. Or simply do what you do with love.

It follows that you need to give without expecting recognition and reciprocation. In giving, you are becoming expansive. And that is its own reward. Indeed, brain scans of people in the act of giving reveal a "warm glow," and this glow gets larger when you are directly giving.[158] So give for the glow, and not for the glory.

Constant giving will also create your capacity for letting-go and sharing. You will feel less insecure when parting with things or even people.

Of course, you don't have to keep giving to the same person! You'll create spoilt brats! But the way to balance that is not to stop giving. Instead, give more by giving to as many people and in as many ways. Give food, money, cheer, hope, kindness, support, positive outlooks, and motivation… Give in the way you want and to whom you want. Don't be conned into giving!

Also, help and nurture those people who, like you, are appreciative and positive. See them as your collaborators. Be there for them.

Giving needn't be seen as superior to taking. We are in any case living-off natural, material and emotional energies in our environment. So accept that you need the energy of others to energize yourself.

In fact, I suggest conscious taking to reduce our (illusory) sense of self-sufficiency. Even when you can do things on your own, it is good to ask others for help. In asking genuinely, you shed a layer of your ego and become natural, while others too get an opportunity to become givers, which will uplift their hearts.

'H' FOR HAPPINESS!

If you want to be happy, there are ways to be so. And if you'd rather wallow in misery, that's possible too! Just know that you can live in energizing ways and give yourself the gift of happy living. Now you have all the means you need. Apply!

Work away your confusions, sing away your pains, laugh away your troubles, and learn from your mistakes. When you fall, rise again, and when you lose, dream again. Trust the loving embrace of the universe. And enjoy the ups and downs of life in the spirit of play.

I summarize key takeaways from the three sections in a brief conclusion.

*Wherever you go, no matter what the weather,
always bring your own sunshine.*
—Anthony J. D'Angelo

TAKEAWAYS

INTEGRATING WITH LIFE

Creative living is a journey of coming closer to your truer self—most aligned with your conscience, most distanced from your ego, mindful of your blessings, forgetful of your animosities, sensitive to others, responsive to your environment and a creator of positive realities.

Our aim here is not to become 'perfect'. Perfection is a call of the ego, not of nature. Like nature, we simply want to evolve and expand with every passing experience, situation, or challenge.

Finally, we are all in the quest of integrating with ourselves, others and our universe. That is when we feel strong and secure. With the software of creative living, you will see, hear, think, imagine, behave, respond and act in ways that help you integrate with the positive energies innate in you and around you. You will become pro-life and make others so!

For recall, I integrate here the creative approaches toward seeing, being and creating.

SECTION I: FOR CREATIVE VISION: SEEING BETTER

I.   See your priorities in clear focus. A lot of confused thinking will go away!

II. See others as part of your larger family. Your feelings toward others become congenial and correct when you imagine a bond of kinship or friendship with them.

III. See with gratitude. When you are more grateful, you are more thoughtful.

IV. See what is possible in a situation. Then what is not possible will not seem such a problem.

V. See with faith in the universe. You'll beget faith in yourself.

VI. See yourself in a bigger role. A lot of small problems will just disappear.

VII. See with passion. You can make the mundane meaningful with your commitment and energy.

VIII. See your mistakes as learning curves. Mull over your new resolves instead of moaning over your past mistakes.

IX. See and visualize pretty pictures with happy endings. Why watch horror films!

X. See and appreciate beauty wherever you find it. You'll gain a positive outlook and trigger the better side in others.

XI. See the strategic potential of space. Seek or create environments to induce relaxation, cause a shift of perception, prime receptivity or inspire the senses.

XII. See like children do. Like them, see possibilities everywhere and create work out of nothing!

XIII. See how you can use visual gestures to help and heal. People will forget what you said but will always remember what you did. Be seen as a friend.

XIV. See(k) role-models and ruminate on them. That's how you will become what you think of becoming and even go beyond your models.

XV. See the brighter side at all times. Even if you can't solve a problem, you can save someone from feeling miserable.

SECTION II: FOR CREATIVE VOICE: BEING BETTER

I.   Be an observer. Watch over your own behavior. Watch the behavior of others. Learn from both!

II.   Be patient. Impatient reactions give rise to imprudent actions. Gradually eliminate them.

III.   Be critical of yourself and accepting of others. Normally we do the reverse!

IV.   Be an example of all that you value. Walk the talk. Only when you lead by example will others get a chance to follow you!

V.   Be cautious of the company you keep. You are more impressionable than you think. Open yourself to positive influences and stay at arm's distance from negative ones.

VI.   Be eager to notice and affirm the good values in others. You will reinforce them and encourage people to live by their better natures. You too will be forced to pace up!

VII.   Be clear about the place and role of different people in your life. The less you expect, the more you will get.

VIII.   Be truthful but careful. Before you express yourself, assess your environment.

IX.   Be more than willing to accommodate. If your brother wants the window seat, give it to him! If your partner wants to try a new restaurant, be game! Lose those little battles that help you win a heart.

X.   Be firm in action instead of being harsh in words. You can always do what you want without hurting others.

XI.   Be quick to regain your calm whenever you lose it. You can see situations better and respond to them better only if you remain cool and collected.

XII.   Be quick to make up and move on. Watch how fast children do it! By being stuck and stubborn, you'll stay where you are. By being open and forgiving, you'll freely move around.

XIII. Be active in taking help from different characters in your life. So when in need of counsel, meet your mentor. When in need of care, meet you mom. When in need of motivation, meet your competitor! Move around to shop for what you need, instead of lamenting your imbalance.

XIV. Be absorbed in your creative vocations. Children attract our attention because they are utterly absorbed in their play. You too will attract the love of the universe, not by playing to the gallery, but by sincere and heartfelt immersion in your work.

XV. Be keenly aware of your inner voice. Follow it no matter how much of a humble pie it makes you eat.

SECTION III: FOR CREATIVE VIGOR: CREATING BETTER

I. Create handy mantras to counter negative feelings. Just like you gush "C'mon, c'mon, you can do it," to an athlete, say likewise to yourself!

II. Create beauty wherever you get space. Otherwise the banal will creep in! Offer a smile, a compliment, a flower, or a word of encouragement. Offer with affection.

III. Create warmth and camaraderie. Make people feel comfortable and cared for.

IV. Create a moment of grace through your forgiveness. Have a forgiveness day!

V. Create a bond with the universe. Connect to it through your prayers, meditation and music.

VI. Create pleasant feelings. Use good words or just your charm!

VII. Create energy in your listening. Be genuinely interested to learn about other worlds and as seen through the eyes of others. Travel freely!

VIII. Create feel-good lines to help yourself out of despair. Even make-believe is great when it makes you believe in yourself!

IX. Create music out of all energies. Remix and remodel whatever material you have!

X. Create a collaborative circle. Just like a symphonic orchestra uplifts the music of the individuals, so too will your creativity multiply through collaboration.

XI. Create new and higher goalposts. Always respond to challenges with your positive values and vision. Stand on a turf that strengthens your spirit.

XII. Create with your heart and soul. Labor with love.

XIII. Create continuously. Start new things when old projects end. Just the way you took classes in the new grade barely after the previous grade's exams!

XIV. Create by emptying yourself of prior creations. That's how new ones will arrive!

XV. Create with peace. Enjoy your creative process. Make the journey satisfying. The destination is just an excuse!

SOME QUESTIONS ANSWERED

During the writing of this book, I responded to a variety of questions around my subject. I present here the answers to some of them, in the hope that they will answer some of your lingering questions as well.

I. **Question:** What is love?

Answer: Love is a positive force of feeling that pushes us out of ourselves and takes us beyond. It makes us want to reach out to someone or something without any apparent reason at all.

However, our excessive expectations narrow the scope of this creative force. No wonder that love leads to tragedies! In fact, a group of teenagers once told me that they understood love as, "**L**ake of tears + **O**cean of sorrow + **V**alley of death + **E**nd of life!"

To get our perspective right, here is an uplifting story to remind us all what true love is all about. In this episode in the Indian epic *Ramayana*, Lord Rama is exiled for fourteen years by his stepmother, as she wants her real son to be crowned the king (which is only possible if the elder brother, Lord Rama, is not there to take up this role that is rightfully due to him). However, this younger (half) brother loves and respects Lord Rama and really wants him to be king, not himself. So upon hearing of the exile orders, he rushes to stop him, making a plea, similar to what most of us might say in such moments. He says: "If you really love me brother, then you will not leave me." It is at this point that their guru, or spiritual guide, gently intervenes and tells the younger brother what true love is all about. He says that when we truly love, we need to think more about the happiness of the other. In this case, Lord Rama's happiness lies in respecting the wishes of his father and mother and thus in accepting the exile. So let us all relearn how to love!

II.   Question: Why do we need to pray?

Answer: Prayer is a way to access your inner most as well as highest feelings. Now if you are asking for a peaceful resolution to a problem, then you indeed value peace above strife. Become aware of such deeper feelings that surface in your state of prayer. Return to your ordinary state with a longing to live by them.

I'd like to share with you an anecdote about Swami Vivekananda. He was a disciple of the great saint Ramakrishna. When Vivekananda's father died, he and his mother were left in great financial difficulty. The poverty and suffering made him question God's benevolence. He asked Ramakrishna why the goddess (Kali) would not relieve her devout disciples of their poverty. Instead of replying, Ramakrishna asked him to ask the divine mother for whatever he yearned for.

It is said that when Vivekananda went to the Kali temple to pray, he felt a surge of extraordinary energy within him. And when he moved his lips to pray, he found himself asking for *bhakti*, *shakti*, and *mukti*, or devotion, strength, and freedom. In his heart of hearts, he wanted alleviation of his spiritual poverty, and not his material poverty. In your prayers thus, you too will come face to face with your truer needs.

III. **Question:** What is god?

Answer: Vedanta considers god as a caring and creative consciousness. That's why Indians see the ultimate source as feminine, because it is inclusive and nurturing. When you too engage in any act of positive creation, preservation and transformation, you align with this cosmic consciousness.

IV. **Question:** How can I drop all fears?

Answer: A guru once told me that there are two kinds of fears: objective fear and subjective fear. Your greater attentiveness and vigilance will take care of your objective fears. For subjective ones, use the means of visualization, mind games, lyrical lies and faith.

V. **Question:** Are our desires 'bad'?

Answer: Sri Sri Ravishankar, an Indian guru, once said in a discourse that when you lightly desire things, your actions become strong. But when you strongly desire to things, your actions become weak." So desire for sure. But do so with openness and playfulness. Patiently work toward nurturing your dreams and desires. Let the fruits come, as they will. They have to come! And sometimes they come in a form and manner, which is even beyond your imagination. Welcome the surprise!

VI. **Question:** Am I a bad person if I am feeling jealous of my colleague's promotion?

Answer: You're just insecure! The way to overcome your insecurity is to participate in another's success. See your friend as your brother or sister. You will really start feeling happy in his or her happiness.

And happiness is not a scare commodity that you have to fight for it. You can access as much happiness as you want! Create it for yourself. Not by envying others, but by getting inspired from them.

VII. Question: What should I do if someone is not responding to my positive efforts?

Answer: Try again, or try elsewhere!

ACKNOWLEDGEMENT

I thank my parents for always understanding my unique path. Their acceptance and love is a source of strength. I thank the dedicated presence of Gowri, my caretaker, who despite being untaught has a most evolved spirit.

I bow in gratitude to many masters and gurus whose lives have been committed to improving our lives. Their teachings continue to deeply inspire my life and influence my work.

I thank art therapist Ikuko Acosta at New York University for the role she played in getting me started on this book. Had it not been for her initial interest in co-writing it, I perhaps wouldn't have had the courage to embark on this journey alone. Even though she had to opt out for personal reasons, her thoughts and case-studies inform the first section of my book.

In November 2009, I visited a few universities in the United States as part of my pre-launch tour. I'd like to especially thank: Mike Ryan at George Washington University; Paul Raushenbush at Princeton University; renowned architects Diana Balmori and Joel Sanders at Yale University; Marty Mauzy and Bruce Jackan at the Ash Institute, Harvard Kennedy School; Deepti Nijhawan, Arundhati Tuli Bannerjee, Alan Brody and Phillip Khoury at MIT; Ikuko Acosta and Tami Herzog at New York University; and Dr. Portia Williams, Samantha Lu and Samira Afzali at Columbia University.

During this very stimulating tour, I met students, staff, research fellows and faculty from a range of cultural backgrounds and academic interests. Initially, I was a bit unsure whether lawyers or architects or scientists would be interested in my subject. Yet, the way every one would warm up to the topic in no time assured me soon enough that no matter where we come from or what our unique situations or temperaments are, we are all seeking ways to improve our relationships and lives. Special thanks to all of them for their attention and affection. My interactions with them truly energized my writing and me.

I thank author and innovator David Pensak for encouraging my work in its very early stages. Later, his wife Karen organized a salon of artists at their residence. I thank all present that evening, especially painter Michele Madeksza from the Delaware Center for Contemporary Arts, and educator and artist Catherine Drabkin from the Delaware College of Art and Design.

I am grateful to Nobel Laureate Dr. Sidney Altman at Yale University for sharing his insights on the need for hard work and discipline in order to meet challenges in personal and public realms. I thank Prof. Joshua Ronen at the Stern School of Business and his wife, Ruth, for their openhearted support.

Special thanks to New-York-based writer and editor, Tracy Hummer; Garima, a doctoral student in the United States; and author Mark Munoz, for their valuable comments the book.

I heartily thank my dear friends Trena Keating and David Pitofsky in New York for being there for me like family. Special thanks to Manmeet and Pushmeet, my brother and sister-in-law in Washington D.C. Their care and the delightful company of their daughter, Meher, made my multi-city tour a most enchanting experience.

I thank all my well wishers and friends for their enthusiasm and encouragement, especially those who shared their struggles and stories with me, with or without realizing that they were triggering my reflections on my topic. I hold a special prayer in my heart for Ritu Singh who proofread the first draft of this book, but is no more among us.

Finally, I am grateful to the Rai Foundation in India for genuinely and generously supporting my book. I thank my agent, Bill Gladstone, for believing in my work. I especially thank Margo Toulouse and my copy editor at Morgan James for their commitment, and David Hancock, founder and CEO of Morgan James, for finding my book worth publishing.

ABOUT THE AUTHOR

Dr Harbeen Arora is a pioneer of *Creative Living* and a compelling speaker who has touched and transformed many lives with her vision of stress-free living. As a mark in the direction, Dr. Arora is in the process of setting up a $100 million 'Creative Habitat', a model site in India where the ethos of creative living comes alive.

She is also the founder and director of HR Communication Foundation, in New Delhi. It is a social enterprise for enabling women in all aspects of their well-being and entrepreneurial talents.

The author has earned her Doctorate from the University of Paris III, Sorbonne Nouvelle; Masters from King's College, University of London and the Royal Academy of Dramatic Art; and Bachelors from Delhi University.

NOTES

INTRODUCTION

1   Allan Wallace (Buddhist scholar), cited in Sharon Begley, *Train Your Mind, Change Your Brain,* New York: Ballantine Books, p. 250.

2   See Nancy C. Andreasen, The Creative Brain: the science of genius, NY: Plume (previously published as The Creating Brain), 2005, p. 30.

3   Cited in Paul Verhaeghen, Jutta Joormann, Rodney Khan, "Why We Sing the Blues: The Relation Between Self-Reflective Rumination, Mood, and Creativity", in Emotion (Journal), Vol. 5, No. 2, 2005, pp. 226–232, available at:: www.apa.org/journals/features/emo52226.pdf, visited November 2008.

PART I: SEEING

1   Rudolf Arnheim, *Visual Thinking.* (Los Angeles and London: University of California Press, 1969), p. 18.

2   Swami Vivekandana, modern Indian spiritualist who brought the teachings of Vedanta to the West, says: "If a person wants to drink milk, he uses a cup as he cannot drink it directly. Idols are nothing but symbols through which divinity can be comprehended." Quote available at: http://aumnamoshivaya.com/Hinduism.htm, visited November 2008.

3   Rudolf Arnheim, *Visual Thinking.* (Los Angeles and London: University of California Press, 1969), p. 254.

4   Cited in Tony Buzan, *Use Your Perfect Memory.* (New York: Plume, 1991), p. 17.

5   In an educational paper presented by Museum of Vision, available at: http://www.aaofoundation.org/what/heritage/Upload/Animal%20Eyes.pdf, visited September 2008.

6   http://www.colormatters.com/market_whycolor.html, visited September 2008.

7   Allan and Barbara Pease, *The Definitive Book of Body Language.* (Bhopal, India: Manjul Publishing House Pvt. Ltd., 2004), p. 166.

8   See Allan and Barbara Pease, *The Definitive Book of Body Language,* p. 67.

9   Jeanna Bryner, "Looking away helps concentration," 12 September 2006, http://www.livescience.com/health/060912_look_away.html.

10   Sharon Begley, *Train Your Mind, Change Your Brain.* (New York: Ballantine Books, 2007), p. 97.

11   Jack Welch with Suzy Welch, "Some things to know if you want it all," in *Mint,* an Indian daily in partnership with WSJ, 26 October 2009, p. 18.

12   Paul Leroux and Peg Corwin, *Visual Selling: Capture the Eye and the Customer Will Follow.* (New Jersey: John Wiley & Sons, 2007), p. 6.

13   http://www.eurekalert.org/pub_releases/2008-03/tu-vte032108.php, visited September 2008.

14   Dr. Aron of SUNY, co-author of the study, cited in a report by Benedict Carey, *The New York Times,* 31 May 2005, available at: http://www.nytimes.com/2005/05/31/health/psychology/31love.html?_r=1&pagewanted=2, visited December 2008.

15   See Shirley Riley, "The Creative Mind," in *Art Therapy: Journal of the American Art Therapy Association,* 21(4), AATA, Inc., 2004, pp. 184–90.

16   Sudhir Kakar, *The Analyst and the Mystic.* (New Delhi: Penguin, 1991). He suggests that the meaning of silence in the West is not quite the same as in the East, p. 77.

17 As personally told by art therapist and NYU professor, Ikuko Acosta, after a workshop with Indian students at the Rai Foundation Colleges, New Delhi, March 2007.

18 Ruth Abraham, *When Words Have Lost Their Meaning.* (Westport, Connecticut: Praeger Publishers), p. 16.

19 Shaun McNiff, *Trust the Process: An Artist's Guide to Letting Go.* (Boston & London: Shambhala Publications, 1998), p. 27.

20 See http://nlpco.com/news/2008/08/08/negative-commands/, visited August 2008.

21 See www.patrickandrews.co.uk/documents/ seekingwholeness_001.pdf, visited August 2008.

22 Frances F. Kaplan, *Art, Science and Art Therapy.* (London: Jessica Kingsley Publishers, 2000), p. 74.

23 See Tyler Cowen, *Discover Your Inner Economist: use incentives to fall in love, survive your next meeting, and motivate your dentist.* (New York: Dutton, 2007), p.60.

24 http://www.businessweek.com/innovate/content/oct2007/ id20071015_340312_page_3 htm, visited September 2008.

25 See Byron Mikellides, "Reflections on Concepts of Aesthetics, Health and Well-being," in *Aesthetics, Well-being and Health* (ed. Birgit Cold), (Hants, England: Ashgate Publishing Limited), p. 179.

26 See Ann Westerman, "Buildings imagined as bodies," in *Aesthetics, Well-being and Health* (ed. Birgit Cold), (Hants, England: Ashgate Publishing Limited), p. 301.

27 See Jason Cato, "Prisons think pink for cells," *Pittsburgh Tribune Review,* 25 December 2007, www.innovations.harvard.edu/ news/76661, visited December 2008.

28 Larry E. Greiner, "Evolution and revolution as organizations grow," in *HBR*, May–June 1998, Reprint 98308.

29 Mihaly Cziksentmihaly, *Creativity: Flow and the Psychology of Discovery and Invention.* (New York: Harper Perrenial, 1997), p. 143, my brackets.

30 Rhonda Byrne, *The Secret*. (London: Simon and Schuster, 2006), p. 91.

31 Juhani Pallasmaa, "The Mind of the Environment," in *Aesthetics, Well-being and Health* (ed. Birgit Cold), (Hants, England: Ashgate Publishing Limited), pp. 218–9.

32 Rikard Küller, "The Architectural Psychology Box of Infinite Knowledge," in *Aesthetics, Well-being and Health* (ed. Birgit Cold), (Hants, England: Ashgate Publishing Limited), p. 136.

33 Swami Sukhbodhananda, *Shiva Sutras: Divine Techniques for Enhancing Effectiveness.*(Mumbai: Jaico Publishing House, 2009), p. 21.

34 www.just-quotes.com.

35 www.brainyquote.com.

36 In Sharon Begley, *Train Your Mind, Change Your Brain*. (New York: Ballantine Books, 2007), p. 70.

37 E. Paul Torrance cited in Rudolf Arnheim, *Visual Thinking*. (Los Angeles and London: University of California Press, 1969), p. 205.

38 Rudolf Arnheim, *Visual Thinking*. (Los Angeles and London: University of California Press, 1969), p. 205.

39 David Pensak with Elizabeth Licorish, *Innovation for Underdogs*. (New Jersey: Career Press, 2008, [Printed in India under license by Perfect Publications, New Delhi]), p. 92.

40 Cited in an article available at: http://www.articlesbase.com/art-and-entertainment-articles/will-learning-to-play-the-piano-or-keyboard-make-you-smarter-688463.html, visited August 2009.

41 Frank R. Wilson, neurologist and author, citing from his book *The Hand*, in a talk titled "The Real Meaning of Hands-on Education," presented at the Institute for Development of Educational Activities (IDEA) Los Angeles, Atlanta, Appleton, Denver—July 1999, text available at: http://www.waldorflibrary.org/Journal_Articles/ RB5101.pdf, visited May 2009. Also see Frank R. Wilson, *The Hand: How Its Use Shapes the Brain, Language, and Human Culture*. (New York: Pantheon Books, 1998).

42 Larry Dossey, *The Extraordinary Healing Power of Ordinary Things*. (New York: Three Rivers Press, 2006), p. 86.

43 Also see a report by Amrita Tripathi, "Art therapy helps child abuse victims," 10 July 2006, http://arttherapy.wordpress.com/2006/07/10/art-therapy-helps-child-abuse-victims/, visited December 2008.

44 See Harriet Wadeson, *Art Therapy Practice: Innovative Approaches with Diverse Populations*. (New York: John Wiley & Sons, 2000), p. 91.

45 See Elena Keller, special psychologist for visually impaired children, "Parents of the visually impaired" Foundation (FRIZ), Moscow, Russia, http://www.icevi-europe.org/cracow2000/proceedings/chapter04/04-17.doc, visited November 2007.

46 See Sharon Begley, *Train Your Mind, Change Your Brain*. (New York: Ballantine Books, 2007), p. 101.

47 As says Joel Pearson, research associate at Vanderbilt University. Research cited in "Mind's eye influences visual perception," July 2008, available at: http://esciencenews.com/articles/2008/07/03/minds.eye.influences.visual.perception, visited May 2009.

48 D. Corydon Hammond, "What is Neurofeedback?," http://www.isnr.org/uploads/whatisnfb.pdf, visited January 2008.

49 See Sharon Begley, *Train Your Mind, Change Your Brain*. (New York: Ballantine Books, 2007), p. 214.

50 Rudolf Arnheim, *Visual Thinking*. (Los Angeles and London: University of California Press, 1969), pp. 18–19.

51 See Rudolf Arnheim, *Visual Thinking*. (Los Angeles and London: University of California Press, 1969), p. 19.

52 As said during his visit to New Delhi in February 2009.

53 Daniel C. Dennett, "How to make mistakes," in John Brockman and Katinka Matson (ed.), *How things are, a science tool-kit for the mind*. (London: United Kingdom: Phoenix, 1995), p. 137.

54   This incident concerns Dr. Christian Dragger, founder and
      chairman, Draggerwerk, a German firm in medical equipment;
      as told and paraphrased by Vinay Rai, former chairman, Usha
      Group, India that once had a joint venture with Draggerwerk.

55   Jonathan S. Feinstein, *The Nature of Creative Development.*
      (Stanford, California: Stanford University Press, 2006), p. 6.

56   Janaki Chaudhry, Vice President, India Growth Team, GE,
      speaking at an event organized by TIE-Delhi, at IHC, New
      Delhi, 8 August 2009.

57   As told by the Maoist militant to journalist Snigdhendu
      Bhattacharya, *Hindustan Times*, New Delhi, Wednesday, June
      10, 2009.

PART II: BEING

1   In "A Dharma Blog," available at: http://zenundertheskin.typepad.
      com/zenreflections/2004/12/index.html, visited May 2008.

2   This incident concerns Dr. Christian Dragger, founder and
      chairman, Draggerwerk, a German firm in medical equipment;
      as told and paraphrased by Vinay Rai, former chairman, Usha
      Group, India that once had a joint venture with Draggerwerk.

3   Report by Annie Murphy Paul, "A Tiny Grimace," *The Week*, 27
      April 2008, p. 43.

4   The boy was called Abhimanyu, the son of the valiant warrior
      Arjuna, and one of the five Pandava brothers who represent
      goodness in the great Indian epic *Mahabharata*. Along with the
      earlier epic *Ramayana*, the *Mahabharata* is considered by Indians
      as not just a dramatic epic but as a historical-philosophical treatise
      that gives us valuable insights on conduct, behavior, and higher
      duties that befit humans. In the epic, Abhimanyu hears, in utero,
      a narration by Lord Krishna that is explaining how to break into
      the Padmavyuham, a peculiar wheel formation used as a war
      tactic. However, since his mother falls asleep while listening to it,
      he only hears and recalls the entry tactic and not the way to exit.

He valiantly breaks into the formation, but unfortunately, he is ensnared and exterminated by seven ace warriors from the enemy-camp in a most horrific way.

5   See Dr. Bruce Lipton, *The Biology of Belief: Unleashing the Power of Consciousness, Matter and Miracles.* (California: Mountain of Love/Elite Books, 2005).

6   See Roland Barthes, *Empire of Signs*, translated from French by Richard Howard. (New York: Hill and Wang, 1982), p. 16. I also cite this example in my doctorate thesis, submitted to University of Paris III, 2005.

7   Steven Gagne, "Understanding Food Energetics," http://www.macrobiotics.co.uk/articles/foodenergetics.htm.

8   Daniel Goleman, "Friends for Life: an emerging biology of emotional healing," http://www.nytimes.com/2006/10/10/health/psychology/10essa.html, 10 October 2006, visited May 2008.

9   See Jacquelyn Ferguson, "Mirror neurons may be why we catch' others' emotional states," 18 March 2008, available at: http://www.news-press.com/apps/pbcs.dll/article?AID=/20080318/HEALTH/803180315/1013/LIFESTYLES, visited April 2008.

10 http://thinkexist.com.

11 Sri Yukteshwar Giri, quote cited at: http://ezinearticles.com/?Thoughts-To-Ponder—77&id=458621, visited August 2009.

12 See Swami Satyananda Saraswati, in Swami Satyasangananda, *Karma Sannyasa.* (Bihar, India: Yoga Publications Trust, 2001 [1984]), p. 131.

13 Prof. Sue Evans, *Wisdom from the Inner Voice*, a publication brought out on the occasion of "Ladies Day 2009", Prasanthi Nilayam, Andhra Pradesh (available in their bookstore).

14 This and many such stories are available in a lovely collection selected and edited by Jamuna Rangachari, *Teaching Stories*, (New Delhi: Magus Media Pvt. Ltd., 2008).

15 See article at: http://www.lifedynamix.com/articles/Inspiration/
    Smile.html, visited August 2008.

16 See article at: http://www.lifedynamix.com/articles/Inspiration/
    Smile.html, visited August 2008.

17 Erich Fried (1921–1988), In his German poem "Ich Liebe
    Dich." English translation by Hasenkatze, available at: http://
    wiki.answers.com/Q/Discuss:Who_is_roy_croft_the_author_of_
    the_poem_Love , visited September 2009.

18 Dr. Stuart Brown, in a talk featured on: http://www.ted.com/
    talks/stuart_brown_says_play_is_more_than_fun_it_s_vital.
    html, visited June 2009.

19 While speaking at an event to launch "Sahabhagi", a campaign
    by the Times Foundation to bring about positive change in
    mindsets in our modern society, held on 28th March 2009, at
    the Ashoka Hotel, New Delhi. I was personally present at the
    event.

20 As seen in a theater-production based on the life of Lal Ded; the
    role of was enacted by Mita Vasisht, and performed during the
    Hungry Heart (Theatre) Festival in New Delhi, 2007.

21 Garry Kasparov, *How Life Imitates Chess* (London: William
    Heinemann, 2007), p. 167.

22 Matthias Rauterberg, Marc Sperisen, and Markus Dätwyler,
    "From Competition to Collaboration through a Shared Social
    Space," paper presented at The 5th East-West International
    Conference, 4-7 July 1995, *http://www.idemployee.id.tue.nl/
    g.w.m.rauterberg/publications/EWHCI95paper.pdf.*

23 Channeling gains, fairly", (India Knowledge@Wharton),
    in *Campaign,* supplement of *Mint,* Indian business daily in
    partnership with *The Wall Street Journal,* 21 April 2008, p. C7.

24 Channeling gains, fairly", (India Knowledge@Wharton),
    in *Campaign,* supplement of *Mint,* Indian business daily in
    partnership with *The Wall Street Journal,* 21 April 2008, p. C7,
    my brackets.

25 In a Bertolt Brecht play, *The Caucasian Chalk Circle*, there is an episode—based on a Chinese (and biblical) legend—where the judge announces a tug-of-war between two women, each claiming to be the real mother of the child. The tug-object is not a rope here, but the real child! Now, as per the ordinary game, the one who would pull the rope, or now child, to her side would be declared the winner', or the real mother. However, that is precisely the judge's stratagem—to figure out the real mother. The real mother will indeed be more caring and will be unable to bear the pain being caused to the child, given the violent yanking. That's what happens. And the one who is gentle to the child is deemed as the real mother.

26 As explained by Professor Alan Brody, founder of the theater program at MIT. Speaking on the topic: "The Idea of Arts in Science and Engineering Education," at *The American Center*, Kolkatta, India, 7 August 2007.

27 http://www.brainyquote.com.

28 Cited in a study by Jesse Ellis and Linda L. Caldwell (Penn State University), "Increasing Youth Voice through Participation in a Recreation-based Teen Center," http://rptsweb.tamu.edu/Faculty/Witt/conpubs/Caldwell%20Teen%20Center.PDF, p. 12, visited June 2008.

29 See Amartya Sen and Jean Drèze, *India: Development and Participation*. Oxford: Oxford University Press, 2002.

30 Sheila Weinstein, "Steel and the grace of creativity," 24 September 2009, article available at: http://www.psychologytoday.com/blog/what-do-i-do-now/200909/steel-and-the-grace-creativity , visited December 2009, my brackets.

31 A talk by author Elizabeth Gilbert, video available at: http://www.ted.com/index.php/talks/elizabeth_gilbert_on_genius.html, visited June 2009.

32   Jack Welch, in his weekly column in *Campaign*, supplement of *Mint*, Indian business daily in partnership with *The Wall Street Journal*, 22 September 2008, C8.

33   Sri Sri Ravishankar, "Radio Art of Living" (604), World Space Satellite Radio, 20 Feb 2008, 7 PM.

PART III: CREATING

1   Robert Roy Britt, "Source of Earth's Hum Revealed, Space Symphony Possible," 26 March 2000, http://www.space.com/ scienceastronomy/planetearth/space_symphony_000323.html, visited December 2008.

2   Cited in Swami Jnanarupananda Saraswati, "Music and the Mind: Infinite Possibilities for Transformation," http://www. yogamag.net/archives/1999/1jan99/music.shtml, visited November 2008.

3   Report dated Sept. 9, 2003, http://science.nasa.gov/headlines/ y2003/09sep_blackholesounds.htm, visited November 2008.

4   See article posted at: http://www.livescience.com/ health/070312_nerves_work.html, visited June 2009.

5   See Barbara J. Crowe, *Music and Soulmaking: Toward a new theory of Music Therapy*. (Lanham, Maryland: Scarecrow Press, Inc., 2004), p. 6.

6   University of Chicago Press Journals, "Oohs And Aahs: Vowel Sounds Affect Our Perceptions Of Products," 13 September 2007, *ScienceDaily*, from http://www.sciencedaily.com- / releases/2007/09/070912130815.htm, Visited August 16, 2009.

7   See J. C. Bose, cited in Paramhansa Yogananda, *Autobiography of a Yogi*. (Kolkata, India: Yogoda Satsanga Society of India, 2006 [1946]), p. 70.

8   Reported in Stephen Kaplan, "The Science of Sound," available at: http://www.sera-soma.com/the_science_of_sound.pdf, visited December 2008.

9   See Barbara J. Crowe, *Music and Soulmaking: Toward a new theory of Music Therapy.* (Lanham, Maryland: Scarecrow Press, Inc., 2004), p. 56.

10   Veda Bharati, "Introduction," *Mantra and Meditation,* (Honesdale, PA: Himalayan International Institute, 1981), p. xxxi.

11   Swami Bhoomananda Tirtha, Vedantic scholar and seer, during his discourses on the *Bhagvad Gita* delivered at the Chinmaya Mission, Lodhi Road, New Delhi, 25–26 November 2008.

12   Swami Bhoomananda Tirtha, Vedantic scholar and seer, during his discourses on the *Bhagvad Gita* delivered at the Chinmaya Mission, Lodhi Road, New Delhi, 25–26 November 2008.

13   Eric Barnhill, "A Special Report for the Cognitive Eurhythmics Community," a book report on, *Rhythm in Psychological, Linguistic, and Musical Processes,* edited by James R. Evans and Manfred Clynes. (Springfield, IL: Charles C. Thomas Press, 1986). Available at: http://cognitive-eurhythmics.com/rhythmbookreport.pdf, visited August 2009.

14   Eric Barnhill, "A Special Report for the Cognitive Eurhythmics Community," a book report *on, Rhythm in Psychological, Linguistic, and Musical Processes,* edited by James R. Evans and Manfred Clynes. (Springfield, IL: Charles C. Thomas Press, 1986). Available at: http://cognitive-eurhythmics.com/rhythmbookreport.pdf, visited August 2009.

15   See Oliver Sacks, *Musicophilia: Tales of Music and the Brain.* (London, UK: Picador, 2007), p. 238.

16   Association for Psychological Science, "Human Brain: Detective of Auditory And Visual Change." Science Daily, 22 January 2008, http://www.sciencedaily.com- / releases/2008/01/080118115432.htm, visited December 2008, my brackets.

17 This higher attentional alertness of the brain could also have come about due to the fact that visuals could always be revisited but sounds, being fleeting, had to be grasped there and then. See Association for Psychological Science, "Human Brain: Detective Of Auditory And Visual Change." *Science Daily*, 22 January 2008, http://www.sciencedaily.com-/releases/2008/01/080118115432.htm, visited December 2008.

18 Alfred A. Tomatis, *The Ear and the Voice*, translated into English by Pierre Sollier and Roberta Prada, (Maryland/Toronto/Oxford: The Scarecrow Press, Inc. 1995), p. 8. (Originally published as L'Oreille et La Voix, Paris: Laffont, 1988), my brackets.

19 In an article, "How Singing Improves Your Health (Even if Other People Shouldn't Hear You Singing)," available at" http://www.sixwise.com/newsletters/06/06/07/how_singing_improves_your_health_even_if_other_people_shouldnt_hear_you_singing.htm, visited December 2008.

20 Cited in Karen Beuerlein, "Enchanted Voices," article available at: http://www.anndyeryoga.com/Enchanted_Voices.pdf, visited July 2008.

21 Inayat Khan, *The Mysticism of Sound*. (Washington, DC: Health Research Books, 1972), p. 76.

22 In a video of the author's talk, available at: http://www.ted.com/talks/philip_zimbardo_prescribes_a_healthy_take_on_time.html, visited June 2009.

23 Alvaro Pascual Leone, "The Brain That Plays Music and Is Changed by It," available at: http://tmslab.org/wp-content/files/PascualLeone_MUSICBRAIN_NYAcadSci.pdf, visited August 2009.

24 See Oliver Sacks, *Musicophilia: Tales of Music and the Brain*. (London, UK: Picador, 2007), p. 94.

25 Karolinska Ins titutet. "Intelligence And Rhythmic Accuracy Go Hand In Hand," *ScienceDaily* 21 April 2008, available at: http://www.sciencedaily.com- /releases/2008/04/080416100459.htm, visited 8 September 2009.

26 Cited by Eric Barnhill, speaking on "Music and Imagination: The Rhythmic Brain," 14 January 2008, edited transcript available at: http://www.philoctetes.org/documents/The%20 Rhythmic%20Brain.pdf, visited August 2009.

27 Judith Lynne Hanna, *To Dance is Human: A Theory of Non-verbal Communication.* (Chicago, USA: University of Chicago Press, 1987 [1979]), p. 111.

28 Work of James W. Fernandez (1966), cited by Judith Lynne Hanna, *To Dance is Human: A Theory of Non-verbal Communication.* (Chicago, USA: University of Chicago Press, 1987 [1979]), p. 112.

29 Reported by Meera Lee Sethi, *The (Real) Sound of Silence*, 18 March 2008, available at: http://www.inklingmagazine.com/ articles/the-real-sound-of-silence/, visited August 2009.

30 Pushpak (1988).

31 Dr. Barry Quinn in an interview cited by author Robert Lawrence Friedman, available at: http://www.remo.com/portal/ pages/health_rhythms/library_article8.html, visited August 2009. Excerpted from Robert Lawrence Friedman, *The Healing Power of the Drum.* (Gilsum, New Hampshire: White Cliffs Media, Inc., 2000).

32 In an interview, 14 Jan 2004, available at: with http://www. rediff.com/news/2004/jan/14inter.htm, visited December 2009.

33 http://www.gaia.com/quotes/yogi_bhajan.

34 http://www.gaia.com/quotes/yogi_bhajan.

35 http://www.musicloversgroup.com/music-quotes-sayings-and-proverbs, visited August 2009.

36 Daniel J. Levitin, *This is Your Brain on Music: The Science of a Human Obsession.* (New York, USA: Dutton, 2006), p. 216, my brackets.

37 See Daniel J. Levitin, *This is Your Brain on Music: The Science of a Human Obsession.* (New York, USA: Dutton, 2006), p. 27.

38 Research of N. Masataka, 1999, reported at: http://www. progressdaily.com/2007/01/, visited November 2008.

39 Daniel J. Levitin, *This is Your Brain on Music: The Science of a Human Obsession.* (New York, USA: Dutton, 2006), p. 43.

40 See Daniel J. Levitin, *This is Your Brain on Music: The Science of a Human Obsession.* (New York, USA: Dutton, 2006), p. 43, my brackets.

41 Cited in Brian Foster, "Einstein and his love of music," January 2005, http://www.pha.jhu.edu/einstein/stuff/einstein&music. pdf, visited August 2009.

42 In *Finding Forrester* (2000) where Sean Connery plays a reclusive genius writer.

43 Released in 2009; Made by Indian actor and social activist Nandita Das.

44 Original lines in Hindi.

45 To be practiced under professional guidance.

46 Swami Sivananda, *Practical Lessons In Yoga.* (Uttaranchal, India: Divine Life Society Publication, 2001). Web edition, available at: http://www.dlshq.org/download/practical.htm, visited December 2008, my brackets.

47 Mikko Sams, professor at the Helsinki University of Technology, in an article reporting the study, available at: http://ybelov. livejournal.com/218181.html, visited August, 2009. This particular study recommends learning languages through audio means.

48 See Gerry Everding's report of a new study by the Dynamic Cognition Laboratory at Washington University in St. Louis., in his article "Readers build vivid mental simulations of narrative situations, brain scans suggest," 26 Jan 2009, available at: http://news-info.wustl.edu/tips/page/normal/13325.html, visited August 2009.

49 Says the character of August Rush, played by Freddie Highmore, in the eponymous film (2007), my brackets.

50 See the compilation of "Compelling Research Findings Regarding the Necessity of Learning a Foreign Language," available at: http://www.power-glide.com/PTA/why_a_second_language.pdf, visited August 2009.

51 See a study reported by Kate Melville, "Move your head to change your mind." 10 July 2003, available at: http://www.scienceagogo.com/news/20030609233203data_trunc_sys.shtml, visited August 2009.

52 Bhootnath (2007).

53 See Connie Tomaino's insights as explained in "Therapist Uses Music to Tune into the Brain," 22-05-08, article available online at: http://www.therapytimes.com/content=0802J84C489EBC86 406040441, visited November 2008.

54 Björn Vickhoff, *A Perspective Theory of Music Perception and Emotion*, Doctoral Dissertation at the University of Gothenburg, 2008, available at: http://gupea.ub.gu.se/dspace/bitstream/2077/9604/2/Vickhoff_inlaga.pdf, p. 143, visited August 2009.

55 Cited by Martin Spaink, "Some reflections on the use of Electronic Substitute Tanpura and the intricacies of proper tanpura tuning," 2003, available at: http://www.medieval.org/music/world/martin_est.html, visited August 2009, my brackets.

56 Daniel Barenboim, "In the beginning was sound," Reith Lectures 2006, (Lecture 1), 7 April 2006, http://www.bbc.co.uk/radio4/reith2006/lecture2.shtml, visited July 2008.

57 Alvaro Pascual Leone, "The Brain That Plays Music And Is Changed By It," available at: http://tmslab.org/wp-content/files/ PascualLeone_MUSICBRAIN_ NYAcadSci.pdf, visited August 2009.

58 Dr. Robert S. Root-Bernstein, cited in an article by Richard A. Knox, "In Music, Whole Brain Gets Involved," 23 November 1992, available at: http://www.fhponline.org/pubs/in_music. html, visited August 2009.

59 Also See Vanderbilt University. "Musicians Use Both Sides Of Their Brains More Frequently Than Average People." *ScienceDaily* 3 October 2008. Available at: http://www. sciencedaily.com- /releases/2008/10/081002172542.htm, visited June 2009.

60 See Northwestern University, "Musicians Have Biological Advantage in Identifying Emotion In Sound," 5 March 2009. *ScienceDaily*, available at: http://www.sciencedaily.com- / releases/2009/03/090303161427.htm, visited September 2009.

61 In an interview with Gowri Ramnarayan, 8 January 20, the Hindu, available at: http://www.hindu.com/mag/2006/01/08/ stories/2006010800010100.htm, visited October 2008.

62 The artist is Itzhak Perlman.

63 As said by Rabbi Jack Reimer who was in the audience that evening. Cited by Larry Dossey, *The Extraordinary Healing Power of Ordinary Things.* (New York: Three Rivers Press, 2006), p. 113.

64 Larry Dossey, *The Extraordinary Healing Power of Ordinary Things*, (New York: Three Rivers Press, 2006), p. 114.

65 Cited by Monika Halan, "Warm Glow of Giving to Appease Conscience," *Mint*, Indian business daily in partnership with *The Wall Street Journal* 14 October 2009, p.6.

BUY A SHARE OF THE FUTURE IN YOUR COMMUNITY

These certificates make great holiday, graduation and birthday gifts that can be personalized with the recipient's name. The cost of one S.H.A.R.E. or one square foot is $54.17. The personalized certificate is suitable for framing and will state the number of shares purchased and the amount of each share, as well as the recipient's name. The home that you participate in "building" will last for many years and will continue to grow in value.

Here is a sample SHARE certificate:

THIS CERTIFIES THAT
YOUR NAME HERE
HAS INVESTED IN A HOME FOR A DESERVING FAMILY

1985-2005
TWENTY YEARS OF BUILDING FUTURES IN OUR
COMMUNITY ONE HOME AT A TIME

1200 SQUARE FOOT HOUSE @ $65,000 = $54.17 PER SQUARE FOOT
This certificate represents a tax deductible donation. It has no cash value.

YES, I WOULD LIKE TO HELP!

I support the work that Habitat for Humanity does and I want to be part of the excitement! As a donor, I will receive periodic updates on your construction activities but, more importantly, I know my gift will help a family in our community realize the dream of homeownership. **I would like to SHARE in your efforts against substandard housing in my community!** *(Please print below)*

PLEASE SEND ME _____ SHARES at $54.17 EACH = $ $_____

In Honor Of: _____

Occasion: (Circle One) HOLIDAY   BIRTHDAY   ANNIVERSARY

OTHER: _____

Address of Recipient: _____

Gift From: _____ *Donor Address:* _____

Donor Email: _____

I AM ENCLOSING A CHECK FOR $ $_____ PAYABLE TO HABITAT FOR HUMANITY OR PLEASE CHARGE MY VISA OR MASTERCARD *(CIRCLE ONE)*

Card Number _____ Expiration Date: _____

Name as it appears on Credit Card _____ Charge Amount $ _____

Signature _____

Billing Address _____

Telephone # Day _____ Eve _____

PLEASE NOTE: Your contribution is tax-deductible to the fullest extent allowed by law.
Habitat for Humanity • P.O. Box 1443 • Newport News, VA 23601 • 757-596-5553
www.HelpHabitatforHumanity.org

Printed in the USA
CPSIA information can be obtained
at www.ICGtesting.com
JSHW082201140824
68134JS00014B/356